# THE ATLAS OF
# GLOBAL
# CHANGE

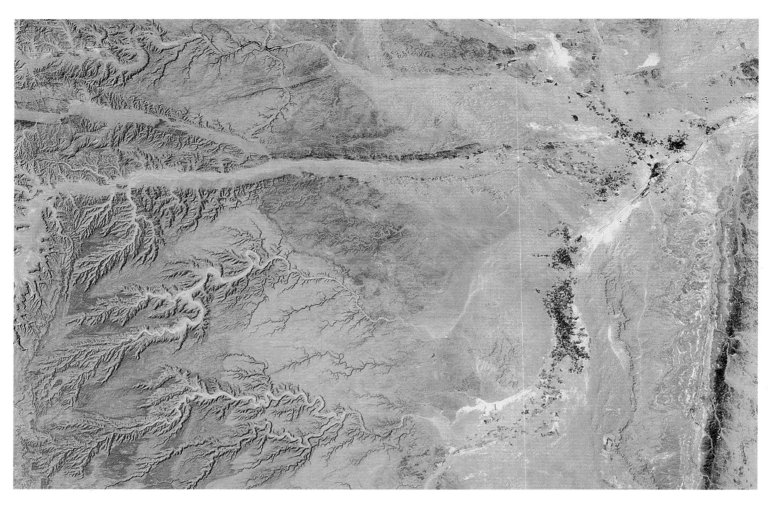

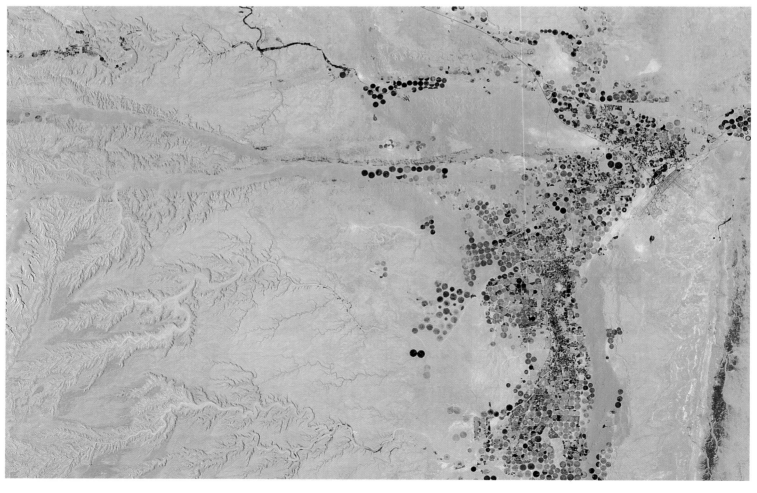

# THE ATLAS OF GLOBAL CHANGE

Edited by Lothar Beckel

Macmillan Library Reference USA
Simon & Schuster Macmillan
New York
Prentice Hall International
London  Mexico City  New Delhi  Singapore
Sydney  Toronto

**The Authors**
Univ.-Doz. Dr. Lothar Beckel, Bad Ischl (pages 8–11, 36–41)
Dr. Ambros Brucker, Lochham (pages 12–19, 22–25, 28–35, 44/45, 48–53, 56–61, 64–75, 84–87, 90/91, 96–99,
102/103, 108–111, 120/121, 122–141, 146/147, 152/153)
Michael Neumann-Adrian, Feldafing (pages 2–7)
Prof. Dr. Dr. Ulrich Pietrusky, Ortenburg (pages 26/27, 104–107, 118/119, 122/123)
Dr. Bernhard Raster, Inning (pages 42/43, 46/47, 54/55, 80–83, 88/89, 92–95, 112–117, 142/143, 148/149)
Dr. Alexander Siegmund, Mannheim (pages 62/63)

Frontispiece: Two views of the vicinity of al-Harg Oasis in Saudi Arabia: the upper satellite image shows the oasis in 1973; the lower photo depicts its status in 1989. The changes that occurred at the oasis during this 16-year period are readily discernible. Formerly small, densely clustered oasis with the majority of its fertile areas concentrated at sites close to groundwater wells, al-Harg has been developed into an extensive tract of cultivated fields, wrest from the desert through modern irrigation technology using circular sprinkler systems. (See also pages 114/115.)

MACMILLAN
A Simon & Schuster Macmillan Company
1633 Broadway
New York, NY 10019

First United States edition 1998

Library of Congress Cataloging-in-Publication Data
Global change.   English.
The atlas of global change / edited by Lothar Beckel.
p.   cm.
Includes index.
ISBN 0-02-864956-7
1. Global environmental change.   2 Nature-Effect of human beings on.   I. Beckel, Lothar.   II. Title.
GE149.G4813   1998   98-2955
550-dc21   CIP
Editor-in-Chief: Carlo Lauer, Falk-Verlag AG, Munich
Project Director: Karl-Heinz Schuster, Falk-Verlag AG, Munich
Translation: Howard Fine, Beust Verlag Gaia Text GmbH, Munich
Editor: Raphaela Moczynski, Munich
Keyline: Hubert K. Hepfinger, Freising
Cover Design: Judy Kahn
Repro Director: Wolfgang Mudrak, Falk-Verlag AG, Munich
Cartography: Geo Data GmbH & Co. KG, Stuttgart

Selection and Processing of Data in the Satellite Photo Maps: Dipl.-Geogr. Jürgen Janoth, Geospace, Beckel Satellitenbilddaten GmbH, Salzburg
Digital Treatment of Satellite Photos: Dr. Markus Eisl, Dipl.-Geogr. Jürgen Janoth, Dipl.-Ing. Gerald Mansberger, Gerald Ziegler, Geospace, Beckel Satellitenbilddaten GmbH, Salzburg
GIS-Implementations: Mag. Ursula Empl, Franz Gütl, Dipl.-Geogr. Jürgen Janoth, Dipl.-Ing. Werner Schnetzer, Geospace, Beckel Satellitenbilddaten GmbH, Salzburg

Realisation of the Layout and Typesetting: Typographischer Betrieb Walter Biering, Hans Numberger, Munich
Reproduction: Worldscan, Munich
General Manufacture: Interdruck Graphischer Großbetrieb GmbH, Hohenossig

Printed in Germany

# Contents

*Algeria: fissured tassili in the Sahara*

*The delta at the mouth of the Mississippi River in the Gulf of Mexico*

*Cloud vortices above Jan Mayen in the North Atlantic*

*Hurricane "Fefa" over the Pacific in August 1991*

# Foreword

"Global Change," "Think Globally – Act Locally," "One Earth – One Environment," "Global Village," "globalization," and other buzzwords are now no longer found only in the vocabulary of reformers who urge mankind to "rethink things," but have long since found their way into popular discourse.

Words and phrases like these express the worldwide realization that conditions on planet Earth are changing at an increasingly rapid pace. The growth and mobility of human populations, the structure of the economy, and cultural and political situations are a few of the many factors involved in these mutually interdependent changes. Essential causes can be discerned, among other places, in the increasingly close-knit fabric of the global economic network, in the educational and scientific explosions, in the apparent omnipotence of technology, in the speed of data and information transfer, and in the liberation of nearly all cultures from old structures. The results are pressures on the natural resources upon which our lives depend – pressures which have become nearly impossible to comprehend and entirely impossible to control.

It is a question of education, of understanding, of the heart, and hence of the ego: To what degree are we willing to dedicate ourselves to preserving our miraculous Blue Planet and thus also safeguarding our own future? Or will we merely parrot fashionable phrases and continue to utter the aforementioned buzzwords?

What is the cause of the increasingly acute concern about our Earth? What underlies the perception that living conditions are deteriorating everywhere, that the natural world in which we live and upon which we depend is no longer healthy, that our Spaceship Earth is an exceedingly vulnerable and closed system, surrounded by a thin layer of highly delicate and absolutely life-essential atmosphere, clad with an even thinner layer of soil which is the source of our food and water – that most vital fluid which has already grown scarce in many regions? These assertions are not solely derived from heightened individual awareness that problems exist, but also stem – conversely – from public discussions, especially in the mass media.

Aerospace travel, a technology whose practicality and usefulness have often been questioned, is an essential component in these realizations and in their objective quantification. Only space travel enables us to view the Earth from outside, from the great distance needed to achieve an adequate perspective on global problems. Space travel lets us see the whole planet, helps us realize that our Earth is an extremely delicate organism, and allows us to determine whether the changes we detect are due to natural, cyclical variations or are in fact catastrophes brought about by human actions. The results of these observations can unveil new possibilities for solving problems and raising consciousness.

Johannes Koren, who devoted one of his books to the theme of regional aerial photographs, writes: "Only by stepping away can we draw closer to comprehension." And satellite photographs can serve as a powerful and effective instrument for gaining precisely this global perspective.

The intention of this atlas is to foster the growth of consciousness and sharpen our understanding of natural processes and of the consequences of human interventions in the natural environment. It also endeavors to convey the fascination of gazing down from space onto the Earth below and admiring its astonishing diversity of landscapes, structures, forms, and colors.

The notion which ultimately resulted in this atlas was first conceived during a meeting of the European Space Agency. Members of the delegation from the Canada Center of Remote Sensing (CCRS) presented their plan for "Geoscope," an "interactive global change encyclopedia." The idea was to take the results of global and regional, space-based, earth-observation research from around the world, assemble them on a single digital information-bearing medium, and thus make that data widely accessible to the general public. The suggestion of presenting this digital information in book form was made by a member of the German delegation, Prof. Rudolf Winter, who has since become director of the Space Application Institute at the European Commission's Joint Research Center.

The CCRS immediately declared its willingness to provide the relevant material, and Geospace in Salzburg, Austria, took upon itself the task of processing it. Subsequent months saw the development of an intensive and fruitful collaboration between Geospace and the CCRS, especially with Josef Cihlar and Anne Botman, who took charge of CCRS's liaison with the "Geoscope" project. Many things which were not amenable to transfer into the print medium or which would have exceeded the scope of the book were left out, other things were added, and gradually the atlas began to take shape as an independent project in its own right.

Hundreds of hours of computer work using digital imagery processing, digital cartography, and geographic information systems were required to bring the digital information into reproducible form. That task was performed in an exemplary fashion by Geospace team members Jürgen Janoth (cartographic design), Gerald Mansberger, and Gerald Ziegler (image processing). Satellite data mosaics created by Tom van Sant and Bob Stacey provided the basis for global depictions. ESA, EOSAT, Eurimage, and Spot Image supplied data for depictions of individual regions.

The entire project would never have become a reality without the generous support provided by Austria's Federal Ministry for Science and Research in Vienna within the framework of a cooperative agreement with Canada. Engineer Otto Zellhofer, head of a section within a department of that ministry, was responsible for the project.

But what would have been the use of all this effort without a publisher? This atlas would have never been born. Many years of cordial collaboration, tried and tested while creating numerous books, proved its worth here as Prisma Verlag of Munich, Germany, and especially its director, Carlo Lauer, and its editor, Karl-Heinz Schuster, once again gave their unflagging support to the project. Without their verve and their bibliophile enthusiasm, this volume would never have become the one which you, the reader, now hold in your hands.

In my capacity as its editor, I would like to express my particular debt of gratitude to the aforementioned cooperative partners, to the text authors whose names appear on page four, and to all the other people whose labor and contributions helped to create this unique atlas. And to you, the reader, I wish many stimulating hours of discovery and reading pleasure.

Salzburg, Austria, July 1996                    Dr. Lothar Beckel

# THE ATLAS OF
# GLOBAL
# CHANGE

# Humanity and Our Spaceship Earth

Back in the 1960s and 70s, the first Russians and Americans lifted off in Vostok and Apollo on missions around the Earth and to the moon. It was then that some of the earthlings began to realize that our planet itself was a kind of spaceship. And we are all aboard this same spaceship together. American scientist Barbara Ward described the new attitude: "Modern science and technology have created such a close-knit web of communication, transportation, economic dependency, and potential for destruction that the planet Earth on its journey through the infinite has now acquired the intimacy, unity and vulnerability of a spaceship."

Perhaps the world has always been a village. But no human being had ever seen the global village from the perspective of the stars. Technology is extremely efficient at shortening distances and accelerating connections. The ability to take aerial photos from balloons and airplanes was only the first big step toward gaining an overview.

The unceasing flood of images transmitted from satellite cameras created a new transcontinental or even global quality. These images, which we could only dream

*The planet is already very old and the era of human existence is very brief, as is the span of time during which "higher" forms of life have been in existence. The first single-celled organisms appeared in the oceans during the Earth's first billion years. Dry land did not become a habitat for plants and animals until the last tenth of the Earth's history.*

about a few decades ago, show the planet by day and by night against the background of space (even at night, the globe is not veiled in impenetrable darkness, see pp. 14–15). They show the summer as it dries out gigantic regions around the world, and the winter as it wreathes the higher latitudes of our planet in blankets of snow (pp. 64–65 and pp. 96–97).

The longer one gazes at these pictures, at the coastlines, mountains, and continents, the more one feels as if one were in a spaceship flying in an orbit around the Earth. Even the computer-generated false colors showing the relief of the continents (pp. 20–21) reveal the beauty of the "Blue Planet," its diversity, and the complexity of the land-and-water design as it has evolved over unimaginably long eons. In their mind's eyes, much-traveled people can also see the Earth's landscapes and cities, the foreign places that have become familiar to them, and the distant sites they yearn to visit.

Not just since yesterday does Homo sapiens know that our home planet is like a grain of sand in the Milky Way, which measures 100,000 light-years in diameter. Each light-year, we recall, corresponds to a distance of nearly 6.2 trillion or 6,200 billion miles (10 trillion or 10,000 billion kilometers). Nowadays, satellite cameras are bringing us tremendous insights into planetary cycles and interconnections. One example that we can see on our TVs every

day is the weather map. Predictions have become more reliable, and because errors are less frequent, meteorologists now dare to predict the weather several days in advance.

## Why Satellite Cameras Pay for Themselves

The example of the television weather map is only apparently mundane and insignificant because climate is a dominant factor determining the future well-being or misery of the Earth's population. It's also critical to know the causes of climatic change. Unlike manned space travel, where the ratio between cost and benefit continues to be disappointing, the expense of taking satellite photos of clouds and ocean currents, forests and deserts has already paid for itself.

The research needs are likewise gigantic – to learn about the past and to prepare humanity for the future. Historians of climate cannot convincingly explain what caused the ice ages nor have they been able to resolve their arguments about the warming of the Earth's atmosphere – the so-called climatic catastrophe.

It could be misleading to talk about "Spaceship Earth," since this might lead to the assumption that scientists comprehend our planet's networked systems just as well as they understand the construction plans of a rocket or space station. Not long ago,

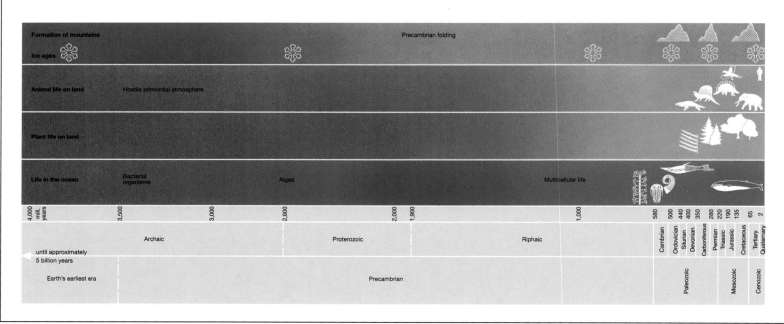

*The Earth – a reservoir of heat. Around the world, some 500 volcanoes spew molten lava, lapilli (stone), and ash, at shorter or longer intervals. Kilauea on Hawaii is one of the "shield volcanoes" that ejects less viscous lava that solidifies into gentle slopes.*

climatic researcher Hans-Joachim Schellnhuber in Potsdam, Germany, made this laconic comment about anthropogenic, industrial "global change": "Our plane has already taken off. We just don't know how to fly it."

### How Long Are Four-and-a-Half Billion Years?

Astonishment about the planet Earth is not likely to end soon. Most astronomers now believe that dust and gas were present at the beginning. In the 1950s, German physicist and philosopher Carl Friedrich von Weizsäcker described the Earth's genesis, when interactions between matter, gravity, centrifugal force, and heat gradually transformed a rotating primal cloud into our sun and its planets. As gravity condensed the interstellar material, temperatures increased dramatically, and this in turn triggered nuclear fusion. According to other astronomers, this fusion released gigantic amounts of energy; eruptions of solar gases created the nine planets.*

Or did it all happen differently? It's a good idea to regard astronomers' theories as just that – only theories. Did the interstellar cloud of dust and gas become a flattened, rotating disk? Over millions of years, this disk could have evolved into a center with concentric rings; countless collisions between meteorites might have led to the creation of the planets. Support for this notion can be derived from the fact that all of the planets' orbits (except Pluto's) lie in

very nearly the same plane and this plane is identical with that of the sun's equator.

Theories about the age of the Earth are a good example of just how volatile the research situation still is. Around 1950, Weizsäcker used the "radioactive clock" (determined by the breakdown of uranium atoms' nuclei) to calculate the age of the Earth at about two billion years. Today, most scientists believe that our planet is more than twice that age: the Earth's geological history began about 4.5 billion years ago; its solid crust formed during its first one-and-a-half billion years; and its oldest rocks formed about 3.6 billion years ago.

Here's a thought-experiment to help you conceive of a 50,000-year time period. That's approximately how long it's been since the first appearance of our earliest direct ancestors in the Homo sapiens group, the creatures whom scientists (perhaps in a flight of arrogant self-aggrandizement) named Homo sapiens sapiens – the wise and sapient humans. If we reduce the Earth's 4.5-billion-year past to the span of one year, then Homo sapiens sapiens' 50,000-year history shrinks to a mere six minutes.

*\* The solar system's nine planets are divided into those that are near and those that are far from the sun. Those nearest the sun (Mercury, Venus, Earth and Mars) have a greater percentage of heavy elements in their compositions than those located on more distant orbits (the giant Jupiter, Saturn, Uranus, Neptune, and Pluto, which was not discovered until 1930).*

### The Egg Full of Embers and Tension

Despite all these billions of years, the Earth still hasn't achieved inner stability, and no end to the unrest is in sight. Beneath the seemingly reliable crust – a layer of rock measuring 19 miles (30 kilometers) in thickness under the continents, 43 miles (70 kilometers) under the folded mountain ranges, and only 4 to 8 miles (7 to 13 kilometers) under the oceans – lies the Earth's mantle: approximately 1,800 miles (2,900 kilometers) thick and up to 3,600 degrees Fahrenheit (2,000 degrees Celsius) hot. We know much less about the depths of the Earth than we know about outer space. Temperatures may rise as high as 7,200 degrees Fahrenheit (4,000 degrees Celsius) in the Earth's core, and its nickel-iron substance may well be liquified in the outer core, greatly condensed and solid in the inner core.

Heat alone isn't the only reason for the Earth's restlessness, nor is it the sole cause of earthquakes and volcanic eruptions. Mighty internal forces are at work building the Earth's crust. Geographers use the words "endogenous forces" and "tectonics." The red and yellow dots on the map of "Earthquakes and Volcanism" (red for volcanoes, yellow for so-called hot spots where heat is conducted to the surface, pp. 28–29) show the Earth's high-risk zones. The strongest earthquakes are almost always caused by movements of the huge plates that comprise the Earth's crust. These plates, in turn, are moved by forces within the mantle. Our map follows the

Mercalli scale of earthquake intensity: the most seriously jeopardized zones are shown in violet, which indicates regions prone to devastating quakes with intensities of grade 9 or higher. Earthquakes can also be caused by human activities, for example, by the flooding of a huge reservoir.

Humankind is no longer helplessly vulnerable to volcanic eruptions and earthquakes. In the most gravely endangered regions (e.g., California, Japan, and China), scientists' predictions of imminent quakes have already been able to prevent catastrophes by warning the inhabitants to evacuate the region before disaster strikes.

## Primal Ocean and Primal Continents

A person who lived during the Christian Middle Ages would have no idea what the concept "global change" could possibly mean. According to Genesis, the first chapter in the Bible, God created the land and sea from primordial waters, "and He saw that it was good." By the seventh day, the labors of creation were complete, and the face of the Earth would not change again until the Apocalypse. The Christian West arrogantly believed that man was the definitive crown of creation, the Earth a flat disk and the center of the world, the sun a mere satellite; even educated Occidentals knew nothing about the discoveries of the ancient Greek astronomers and refused to accept variant opinions voiced by then-contemporary geniuses.

Even today, some Christian fundamentalists refuse to accept the theories of Johannes Kepler and Galileo Galilei, or to

*How did the continents and oceans arrive at their present forms? Alfred Wegener (1880-1930) answered that question with the theory of continental drift described in his book* The Genesis of the Continents and Oceans.

believe that living beings evolve – a theory Charles Darwin first described and that has since been repeatedly proved. During the first third of the 20th century, even expert geologists scoffed at the theory of "continental drift" – one of the most vivid examples of incessant global change.

Geophysicist and polar explorer Alfred Wegener from Berlin undertook three expeditions to Greenland (he died in 1930 during the last of those ventures) to conduct research into arctic ice and continental drift. The striking way in which the coastlines on either side of the Atlantic Ocean seem to "fit" into one another had given rise to a host of theories about the possible origins of the continents. Wegener's theory of continental drift mustered numerous geological proofs and abundant theoretical arguments to win over competing theories. As the continents creep at a snail's pace, floating like vast plates of ice, they leave oceans in their wake and push up mountain ranges ahead of them.

One of the most astonishing proofs of plate tectonics is the almost 44,000-mile-long (70,000-kilometer-long) system of mid-ocean faults that has been researched since the 1960s (pp. 24–25). Highly accurate measurements showed that the seafloor is spreading along these faults. How is this possible? While new crust is forming in the depths of the oceans, old crust is shoved down beneath the edges of the continents, which creates earthquake "nurseries" deep below the coastal regions.

Wegener assumed that the present-day continents arose from a single primordial landmass he named "Pangaia" or "All-Earth." Later, it seemed more likely that there had actually been two protocontinents, Laurasia in the north and Gondwana in the south. Temperature gradients between the Earth's core and its surface seem to be the source of energy that causes continental drift. Today, the continents continue to change their positions by several inches each year.

## Slowness and Growing Acceleration

There's a fairy tale about a diamond mountain and a bird that comes once every thousand years to sharpen its beak by rubbing it against that mountain. When the diamond mountain is entirely worn away, one second of eternity will have passed. The tale is poetic, but nonetheless true: it aptly (but unscientifically) expresses an awareness of the slowness of global change.

The formation of the continents was no doubt one of the grandest of all global changes. But there are other comparably mighty and similarly slow processes, like the uplifting of mountains or their removal

*Extinct for reasons that have not yet been explained, the dinosaurs live on in our imagination, in books and films, and as picturesque dwellers at leisure parks and gardens like this heavyweight Diplodocus at Kleinwelka Dinosaur Park near Bautzen in Saxony (Germany).*

by erosion. Slow changes and long stretches of time have also given rise to our planet's most astonishing phenomenon – the developmental history of life from its beginnings as single-celled marine organisms to the abundance of species of plants and animals that has arisen during more recent geologic eras.

Our planet has been hostess to life for some 3.5 billion years, but more than 3 billion years went by before dry land became suitable as a habitat. Just how much time nature has for "experiments" (which may ultimately fail) becomes evident when we consider the planet's largest fauna thus far. The reign of the great reptiles, the Mesozoic era, lasted for some 150 million years. During the Earth's "middle ages," these dinosaurs (literally "terrible lizards") roamed through moist forests or swam through the oceans as ichthyosaurs ("fish lizards"). What global change put an end to their rule? The answer is still unknown. The largest dinosaur fossil ever found was unearthed in Mexico in 1985: with a length of

peared. Many people associate the word "dinosaur" with the concept of extinction, but this only shows our inability to comprehend the enormous magnitude of these intervals of time.

Tremendous acceleration in the pace of global change characterizes the most recent 10 percent of the Earth's history. New species and new forms of life arose and competed in the struggle for existence. Recurrent ice ages alternated with warmer periods.

Still greater acceleration is evident in the history of human evolution. For millennia, humankind remained within the bounds of its abilities to transform forests into cropland, sail the oceans, and mine gold and silver. Nowadays, the print and electronic media inundate us with so many reports of technological progress and dire catastrophes that many people's faith in tomorrow is succumbing to anxiety about the future.

### The Planet at Night

If satellite cameras are sent aloft over the nighttime Earth and their photos combined to create a single image, one sees a fantastically rich field of sparkling lights (pp. 18–19). One soon realizes that the brightest spots are not necessarily identical with the areas of greatest population density. For example, the Chinese night is still mostly black as ink. Flare-offs at oil fields on the Persian Gulf or in northern Russia make these sites brighter than the urban centers along the eastern coast of North America. Nigel Calder, an American sci-

130 feet (40 meters) and weighing some 99 short tons (90 metric tons), this "Seismosaur" ("earthquake lizard") was larger than a blue whale.

Were the dinosaurs merely a brief episode in the history of life on Earth? If we use the comparison from page 3 where we likened the Earth's past to a single year, we can realize how brief is the span of human culture to date. It took a mere six minutes of that "year" to go from Neanderthal man to the Internet; the dinosaurs, on the other hand, survived almost two full weeks of that "year" before they mysteriously disap-

*The explosive growth of the human population threatens to exceed the Earth's carrying capacity and precipitate a global change that could doom humankind. This severely overloaded small bus is about to flip over. It was photographed on Java by Indonesian photographer Sholihuddin in 1995.*

*War over increasingly valuable resources: Iraqi dictator Saddam Hussein set fire to Kuwaiti oil wells when he was forced to withdraw after his invasion of Kuwait. Ecological pollution caused during the Gulf War of 1990/91 continues to exist long after these fires were extinguished.*

entific journalist, notes that the "night planet" map is less a depiction of population than of wealth: "Each point of light doesn't represent a million people; it represents a million dollars." These nocturnal photos clearly depict the enormous magnitude of the gradient in development and prosperity.

## Conserving Resources: Water, for Example

Becoming well acquainted with the "local history" of our little planet is the first step we earthlings can take toward finding paths into the future. Anyone who doesn't deliberately bury his head in the sand simply must face the facts. Geography, the science of the Earth, is a precondition for "global politics" – a responsible, multinational politics for the entire Earth. And that means: one politics for the necessities of life.

One of the most dismaying photos in this book shows the noxious cloud issuing from burning Kuwaiti oilfields on the Persian Gulf (pp. 48–49). The Iraqi aggressor, who threatened his adversaries with the "mother of all battles" in the winter of 1990/91, caused grave damage to the Gulf's highly fragile ecosystem.

Even in peacetime, the world's oceans are by no means treated as protected natural areas. The Mediterranean Sea is particularly endangered. Industries in countries bordering the Mediterranean pour huge quantities of wastewater into the sea. The toxic effluent becomes visible when it creates a carpet of algae or disgusting foam

that spoils the fun of swimming in the surf, as it did for several summers off the Italian Adriatic coast. (See the photos and map on pp. 88–89. The algal bloom has been colored red in the satellite image.)

Even greater criminal energy is expended to pollute freshwater resources, which comprise only 2 to 3 percent of the planet's water reserves. Water experts at the UN described the pollution, salinification, and shrinking of the Aral Sea as "the century's worst manmade environmental catastrophe." Once nearly one-and-a-half times larger than Switzerland, the Aral Sea has shrunk to half its former size – an inherited burden of Soviet agricultural practice, which thoughtlessly diverted the tributaries that flowed into this vast inland sea.

Two mighty Siberian rivers – the Yenisey and the Ob – have been degraded into

industrial sewers. The Yenisey, and thus also the Arctic Ocean, is jeopardized by radioactivity because, for many decades, the Soviet regime disposed of atomic wastes in an artificial underground lake.

The "blacklist" of technological criminals includes the names of every country. Only the more prosperous nations will be able to repair the damage to nature without outside help. Fortunately, a few examples of ecological renewal do exist. The Rhine River was Europe's largest sewer and a major source of North Sea pollution during the 1970s. Although the Rhine still carries much pollution, the volume of filth has been reduced and fish are returning to its waters. An international program has been established to rehabilitate the mistreated Elbe River. If the program proceeds according to schedule, the river's water should become potable by the year 2010.

## Sources of Energy: Mother Earth, Sister Sun

An artificial pyramid of ice was to have been built to coincide with the 1995 World Climate Conference in Berlin. The plan was to allow the pyramid to melt in the sun as a way of dramatizing the melting of the polar icecaps. The burning of ever-greater amounts of petroleum, natural gas, coal, and wood pollutes the atmosphere, raises global temperatures, and leads to an increase in the elevation of mean sea level (pp. 68–69). And fossil fuel reserves will be exhausted someday anyway. At most, only a few dozen generations will burn fossil-fuel energy; reserves will certainly not last for millennia. Does this mean that humankind will decide to build more atomic reactors

*Large parts of the world's fourth largest inland sea, the Aral Sea in the former Soviet Union, have become a salty swamp. Diversion of water from its tributary rivers (Amu Dar'ya and Syr Dar'ya) to irrigate Kasachi, Turkmenic, and Uzbeki cotton and rice fields caused the surface area to shrink by more than one-third.*

*In the politics of energy too, a tree and the sun are symbols of hope. Combustion of fossil fuels like coal, petroleum, and natural gas uses up irreplaceable natural resources. But as solar cells become increasingly more efficient at making direct use of solar energy, the possibility of an "energy change" is growing increasingly likely.*

and accept the risks of radioactive contamination?

Humanity is obviously challenged to make some global changes of its own. Anyone who looks beyond the short term will no doubt choose sources of energy that will neither become exhausted nor threaten the survival of life itself. Fortunately, nature offers us two such sources: the warmth of the sun and the heat within the Earth. Unfortunately, tapping solar and geothermal energy requires costly initial investments. But in the long run, these expenditures will eventually amortize themselves.

A "solar energy Marshall Plan for eastern Europe" could offer viable alternatives to worn-out Chernobyl-style nuclear reactors. The switch to solar technology could save threatened forests in some developing countries.

## The Time for a "Mental Change"

Every Cassandra sees the imminent catastrophe in her mind's eye, and that vision can make prophets blind to better options. Cassandra could be wrong. The "limits to growth" are not as unalterable as the Club of Rome's famous book *The Limits to Growth* suggested in 1973.

Even without expert knowledge, more and more people are realizing that humankind needs the Earth, but the Earth doesn't need humankind. The narrow ridge between two possible paths into the future is growing narrower every day.

The one path: industrial overuse could ruin the biosphere; radioactive radiation and gene manipulations could irreparably damage genetic material. But the other path is also open – if we have the courage to strive for utopia.

For the first time in history, all of the world's nations have finally joined to conduct collective projects. When famine threatens, help is delivered. Never before have so many people from such widely diverse cultures encountered one another in peace. There really is a chance to create "the best of all possible worlds" – a world without hunger and misery, a world in which every individual is able to pursue happiness and freely develop his or her potential.

The ecological instruments for distributing prosperity have grown dramatically since the "oil crisis" of the Seventies. There's no shortage of prescriptions for combating overpopulation and misery. Knowledge abounds, but wisdom is in short supply. Economic and political will is needed. A "mental change" is overdue.

*Austrian Artist Friedensreich Hundertwasser built the "Hundertwasser House" in Vienna's Löwengasse in 1983/85. It's the fulfillment of the artist's lifelong dream: to create residential architecture that wouldn't be soberly right-angled, but that would be close to nature, colorful, and have greenery on its roof. The city of Vienna helped finance this project as part of its program to provide low-income housing.*

# Earth Observation from Outer Space

The commonly heard saying that "war is the father of all things" seems to prove itself true in many courses of events, and especially in the development of technology. Vast amounts of financial means and human energy have been and still are employed to devise new methods and machines of war. Changes are set into motion by military technology, regardless of whether a war is then actually fought.

Military and strategic considerations also motivated the extensive development of space exploration. Today, however, other goals occupy the foreground, for example, scientific research into the nature of the universe. Humanity is also striving to use technology to repair the widespread damage caused by decades and even centuries of egotism. We are beginning to appreciate the miracle of our world, to recognize its vulnerability, and to comprehend the many intertwining strands that link nature and humankind. Space travel enables us to observe and scrutinize the Earth from outer space.

Aerial surveillance of the Earth began in 1794, shortly after the invention of the hot-air balloon, when French colonel Jean M. J. Coutelle ascended in one to observe the Battle of Fleurance. The first aerial photographs were taken in 1858, when Gaspard Félix Tournachon (also known as the caricaturist Nadar) ascended in a tethered balloon and shot photos of his native Paris.

The first military aerial reconnaissance mission was flown in 1910, when French pilot Marconnet flew over North Africa in a biplane. Large-scale aerial reconnaissance followed shortly thereafter, during the first World War, and assumed much larger proportions in World War II. A parallel development was the growth of missile technology, in which Germany played a leading role.

Reconnaissance technology was further refined during the Cold War and the era of mistrust between East and West. On September 12, 1949, an American reconnaissance aircraft detected traces of a Soviet atomic bomb explosion in the atmosphere. The United States, which had been the world's sole nuclear power until that point, reacted by revising its defense policies, especially with regard to its atomic-weapons program and air force. In order to better monitor the Soviet Union, the United States decided to begin constructing surveillance satellites in February 1955. Plans for such devices had existed since 1946.

Construction of military satellites (the project was code-named "Corona") began in utmost secrecy in March 1955; the first successful launch took place on January 31, 1961. More than one hundred missions were conducted before the program was finally discontinued in May 1972. Cameras equipped with high-resolution lenses had been operating from satellites in orbit around the Earth. After snapping the pictures, they jettisoned their films, which were then intercepted in midair by airplanes.

The Soviet Union launched its first satellite, Sputnik 1, in 1957. The usefulness of both space travel and the observation of Earth from space had been recognized; both programs progressed rapidly thereafter. The first American weather satellite was launched in 1960; ERS 1, the first experimental civilian Earth-observation satellite, followed in 1972. Its purpose was to take inventory of global resources and to document the effects and interventions resulting from human activities. ERS 1's development came at a time during which the first Report of the Club of Rome on the State of Humanity appeared, a publication that drew people's attention to the "limits to growth" and on the nonrenewable nature of the planet's resources. Today, a quarter century after the launching of ERS 1, this fully developed instrument is at the service of science, administration, and business. Although its absence would be unimaginable, the exploitation of its complete capabilities is by no means a matter of course.

Satellite photographs need to be viewed in a special way. Their holistic views can reveal large-scale contexts on Earth, interconnections and interdependencies, as well as the consequences of both natural events and anthropogenic changes. Moreover, taking satellite photographs at regular intervals makes it possible to document cyclical processes, dynamic phenomena, and the reciprocities between these events.

The philosophy behind the exploration of the Earth from outer space is summarized in the diagram on page 10. The background for understanding this diagram is our growing awareness of the effects produced by the present rapid increase in world population. Uncontrolled population growth puts immense pressure on the Earth's natural resources and is inextricably connected with other phenomena such as land usage, industrial growth, communications technology, education, widespread travel, mass transportation, and shipping. Of course, the diagram's two-dimensional format provides a somewhat insufficient depiction of the complex interconnections at work within the entire plexus. As a holographic view of the world maintains, "the part is in

*The rediscovery of the Earth through space travel showed us for the first time the oneness – but also the fragility – of our "Blue Planet."*

*NASA astronauts John W. Young and Robert L. Crippen after the return of the first space shuttle flight on April 14, 1981.*

*On his first voyage in 1492, commanding a small flotilla of three caravels and a crew of 88 men, Christopher Columbus discovered*

*America. It changed the world and ushered in the age of great expeditions. Monument at the embarkation point of his journey in Lisbon's harbor.*

Ground Zero

Aerial reconnaissance during World War I: soon after the development of the first airplanes, "remote reconnaissance" was put to military purposes in World War I. The photo shows a flight by an Austrian biplane over the Dolomite Alps for reconnaissance of Ital- ian military positions in March 1917.

Remote military reconnaissance during the Cold War: on October 24, 1964, the American reconnaissance satellite "Corona" supplied the first pictures of the Lop Nur atomic testing area on the eastern edge of the Tarim Basin in China. Measurement stations were installed along the circular road-way surrounding the center of the test area.

the whole, and the whole is in every part."

If one nevertheless tries to describe the world's system in graphic fashion, it is necessary to introduce additional vectors like space and time. One also needs to consider the individual elements as being mutually associated in three-dimensional space, which we can imagine here as a ball (the planet Earth). This view helps us comprehend the self-contained nature of the system and to see that every factor exists in direct relationship with (and/or is contained within) another factor or phenomenon. These components can be assigned to specific domains, and this arrangement creates three essential spheres:

1. the natural sphere, which consists of abiotic and biotic components;

2. the anthropogenic sphere, which includes all human activities and the various levels of cultural development; and

3. the sphere of contact or collision that inserts itself between the first two spheres and that is variously known as habitat, environment, ecological zone, etc.

This third sphere contains the sum of our resources from the natural and anthropogenic spheres. The effects of positive as well as negative changes become evident here. These consequences can occur on a global, regional (international), or local level. Whatever actions human beings undertake in any of these three spheres triggers a series of changes and/or consequences in nearly all other domains. Sooner or later, these consequences inevitably return to their source in one form or another.

The contents of the natural sphere are listed in hierarchical order: each item is

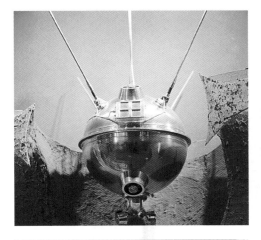

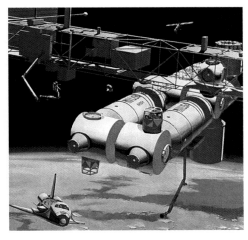

Model of the first artificial Earth satellite, Sputnik I, which the Soviet Union launched into Earth orbit on October 4, 1957. Gemini 6 and Gemini 7 conducted the first success- ful docking maneuver of two manned space ships in December, 1966 (upper right). The first reusable spacecraft, the space shuttle "Columbia," was lifted off from Cape Canaveral, Flori- da, on April 12, 1981. The future in the cosmos: after many years in the planning phase, the International Space Station is soon to become a reality. Participating nations will oper- ate their own research laboratories here. Earth observation will be one of the essential projects of this space station.

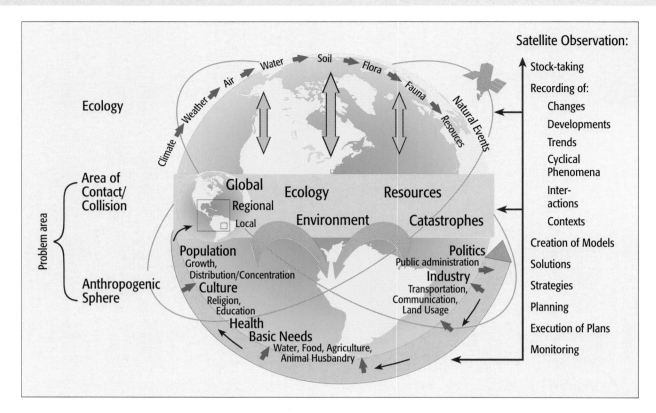

*Earth observation and the global system: nature and man are holistically connected with one another on Earth. Every change and intervening measure that occurs on one level causes reciprocal changes on the other level. Satellites facilitate the observation and analysis of these influences and can assist in the development of potential solutions.*

greatly dependent upon or reciprocally linked to its predecessor (e.g., soil and vegetation). In the anthropogenic sphere, the level of cultural development of the various groups within a population depends upon that group's background, its origins, and its present geographical location; these factors, in turn, influence that group's religion, population density and distribution, education, and upbringing.

A people's health, the kind and extent of their basic necessities such as water, food, and clothing, and the economic activities connected with these necessities are all based on that people's level of cultural development. An advanced economy, together with its long-term effects on natural resources and the environment, can only develop at a higher "level of culture," and this, in turn, often depends on the particular religion present. The extent and depth of encroachments on the environment is proportionate to the strength of a society's economy and the level of its technological development. Next comes the extension of infrastructure, followed by the subsequent expansion of communication. Satellite technology has enabled communications to achieve unprecedented dimensions and to spawn thus far incalculable consequences. Every culture and every system can now be directly influenced from outside in "real time" – and it is in fact influenced, regardless of whether it wants to be or not. As a result, a state of upheaval and new beginnings reigns: old values disappear, but new values frequently do not arise to replace them. Meanwhile, the manmade institution of politics acts and dictates from

above, causing various repercussions throughout the whole system, even as it is itself subject to influences from below.

The system in its entirety becomes comprehensible when it is observed from a distance. Only in this way do individual phenomena, initiatives, and changes organize themselves into patterns. All consequences of human activities in the sense of "global change" are the sums of related actions, thoughts, and initiatives. These occur or appear on a small scale, but are then copied and simultaneously carried out thousands of times elsewhere. This process puts enormous pressure on habitat and the essential conditions it provides for life – a pressure that can ultimately lead to collapse.

Satellites' remote-sensing instruments can be used over shorter or longer intervals of time and their surveillance activities can be periodically repeated to facilitate synoptic, multitemporal, and even hypermedial data comparisons that allow trends on Earth to be clearly recognized. The evaluation of the data takes place from hundreds of different viewpoints; individual results must be mutually correlated according to their interdependency. Information systems created for geographical or other specific purposes are a first step in this direction. Thus far, however, a sufficiently intelligent data-storage system and/or adequate computer memory capacity does not yet exist to allow prompt and correct holistic conclusions to be drawn and to enable further discoveries to be made. First attempts in this direction involve ideas about holographic storage media and fuzzy-logical data processing. Further elucidation of

satellite-photography and data-evaluation techniques is unnecessary here, since these subjects have been adequately described elsewhere.

Many different kinds of satellite images currently exist. These include analog and digital forms; raw data, processed (optimized) data, and interpreted data; photographs made using the visible spectrum of light, or using nearly visible, middle-range and thermal infrared wavelengths; and photos taken using wavelengths in the radar and long-wave microwave range. Satellite images can be made at various levels of resolution, which is defined as the size of the measured ground area corresponding to one scanning point on a digital recording. Resolution currently ranges from 6.6 feet (2 meters) to 3 miles (5 kilometers). In the near future, satellite systems with a power of resolution measuring 3 feet (1 meter) will be available for civilian users.

The leading distributors of satellite images are Spot Image (France), Eurimage (Italy), and Edsat (USA). The latter two also offer a diversity of data originating from other satellite-operating agencies. Data are disseminated via worldwide distribution networks that maintain national contact addresses.

In summary, observation of the Earth from outer space provides a suitable basis for a "Global Geographical Information System" that offers regular surveys of the surface of the Earth, with a high degree of geometrical and thematic detail recognition, for the purpose of taking stock of the Earth's geology, energy-production facilities, infrastructure, morphology, pedology, hydrology, vegetation, land use, agriculture, economy, research about cultural landscapes, land-use planning, environmental protection, and many other purposes:

- makes it possible to detect changes, developments, and trends, as well as to study dynamic meteorological, geophysical, geographical, biological, and hydro-economical phenomena;

- facilitates the identification of interdependencies and interactions between natural and cultivated land, and reveals the consequences of changes and/or human interventions.

Observation of the Earth is the basis for decision-making on local, regional, national, international, continental, and global levels concerning politics, economics, spatial planning, the protection and maintenance of resources and the environment, and many other areas. It provides data needed to create theoretical models and potential solutions, strategies, logistics, and procedural measures. And it allows us to document data about the results of past actions, so that this can be referred to for future decision-making.

Since aerospace travel is high technology, it is also highly innovative. If steered in the proper direction, it can be an even better motive force for the economy than the armaments industry has been, since space travel serves peaceful ends for the general well-being of all humankind. With its "spin-offs" – the diverse applications and advantages derived from it – aerospace technology can replace basic industries that declined in the classic industrialized nations, and can thus relieve our planet from the severe demands that industrialization has imposed upon it.

If we succeed in taking the resources that have thus far been devoted to arms production and reroute them to aerospace travel, perhaps the relevant saying would no longer be "war is the father of all things," but would become – in accord with the equality of the sexes – "space exploration is the mother of all progress." Such a reorientation would offer tremendous impetus for another global change.

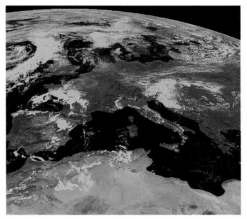

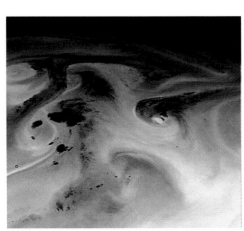

*Weather satellites provide constantly updated information about the Earth's climate and weather. Left, Europe and North Africa as seen from the American satellite NOAA, which orbits the Earth at a height of 870 miles (1,400 kilometers). Satellites observe the Earth with sensors that scan the Earth's surface strip by strip, or with cameras possessing varying degrees of detail resolution. From top to bottom the accompanying single-frame exposures, taken from an altitude of 22,000 miles (36,000 kilometers), are an infrared photograph, which penetrates haze and water vapor; a photograph taken in the spectrum of visible light, which also depicts atmospheric haze; and a photograph taken using wavelengths in the "water vapor absorption band," which shows atmospheric humidity and turbulence in the upper troposphere, 3 to 6 miles (5 to 10 kilometers) above the Earth's surface.*

# The Earth from Space

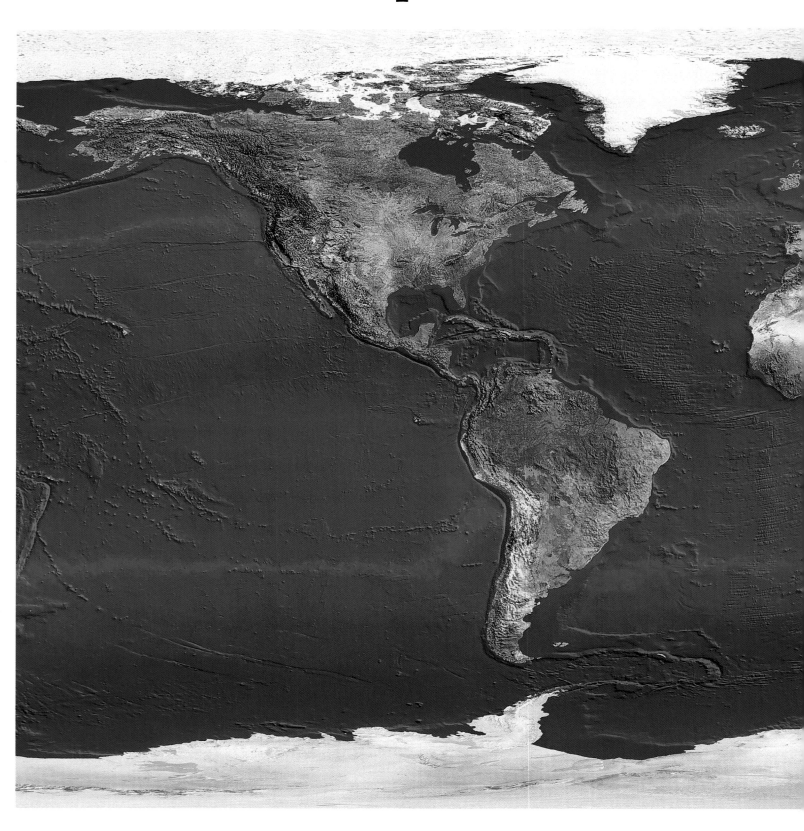

**Relief Forms**

| | | |
|---|---|---|
| high mountains (with glaciers) | lowland | deep-sea trench |
| medium-high mountains | rift valley | undersea ridge |
| highland | river delta | island |
| | continental shelf | |

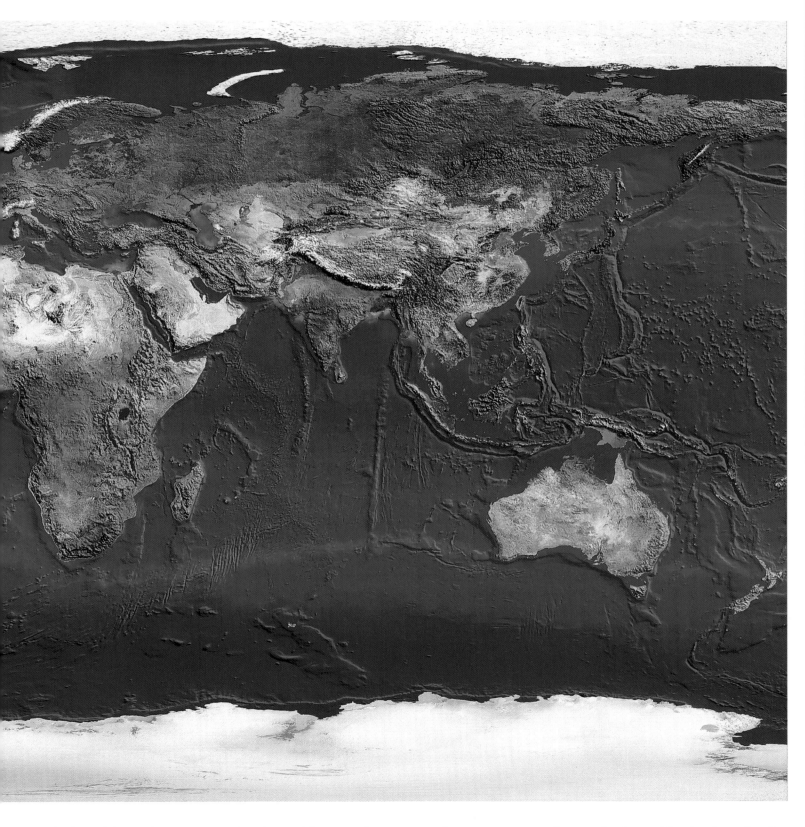

The face of the Earth is unique. Earth is the only planet in our solar system covered by an extensive expanse of water, out of which landmasses rise like gigantic islands. The contiguous continents of Asia, Europe, and Africa together comprise the great eastern landmass; North and South America, connected by a bridge of land and islands, form the western landmass. Another island bridge connects Australia with the Afro-Eurasian landmass. The Southern Antilles and undersea ridges link the Americas with Antarctica. The Pacific Ocean is greater than the total area of all the Earth's landmasses.

# The Earth in the Changing Times o

4:00 a.m.
CET

8:00 a.m.
CET

4:00 p.m.
CET

The Earth rotates about its own axis "toward the sun," that is, from west to east. Because the Meteosat weather satellite orbits the Earth at the same speed at which the Earth rotates around its axis, Meteosat remains geostationary: it always hovers above the same point, namely the intersection of the prime meridian and the Equator. At half-hour intervals, Meteosat supplies images of the same half of the globe; these photos show changes in lighting conditions as seen from the satellite's unchanging vantage point.

At 4:00 a.m. Central European Time (CET), morning twilight has begun to illuminate Turkey and the Somali Peninsula in the extreme eastern part of Africa. The sun has already risen over the Arabian Peninsula, but the rest of Africa is still shrouded in darkness. By 12:00 noon CET, the zone of morning twilight has crossed all of Africa and the Atlantic. At 4:00 p.m. CET, night has fallen over eastern and southern Africa. Because these photos were taken during the Northern Hemisphere's summer, the southern polar region remains immersed in the shadows of night all day.

# Day

12:00 noon
CET

8:00 p.m.
CET

One striking feature in this series of images is the nearly ideal symmetric arrangement of climatic and wind zones as shown by the positions of the clouds. The inner tropical convergence zones with their towering thunderheads are visible on either side of the Equator; south and north of these zones lie the nearly cloudless, subtropical, high-pressure zones of the horse latitudes with their northeast and southeast trade winds. Adjacent to these zones, at still higher latitudes, lie the zones of westerly winds with their cyclones and anticyclones, here including South Africa. The lighting conditions and northward shift of the belts of wind suggest that these photos were taken during the Northern Hemisphere's summer.

This sequence of images clearly documents the dynamism of atmospheric circulation. Enormous towers of clouds begin to form at midday, mainly in the Inner Tropics, but also over the mountains of the central Sahara; by late afternoon, these clouds have conjoined to cover extensive areas.

# The Earth in the Changing Seasons

Spring

Autumn

The changing of the seasons is caused by the inclination of the Earth's axis in relation to the Earth's elliptical orbit around the sun. Since the Earth crosses aphelion (its farthest distance from the sun, 1-3-5) during the Northern Hemisphere's summer, it needs somewhat more time to traverse this portion of the orbital ellipse than it does during the six months of the Northern Hemisphere's winter, when it moves through its perihelion (5-7-1). Hence, according to the calendar, autumn in the Northern Hemisphere doesn't begin until September 23.

At noon on March 21 and September 23, the sun is located directly above the Equator (1, 5); day and night are equally long (2, 6); the North and South Poles are equidistant from the sun. According to the calendar, these are the dates when spring and autumn begin in the Northern Hemisphere, and autumn and spring commence in the Southern Hemisphere. When the sun is situated directly above the northern Tropic of Cancer (3), summer prevails in the Northern Hemisphere, while the Southern Hemisphere experiences its win-

Summer

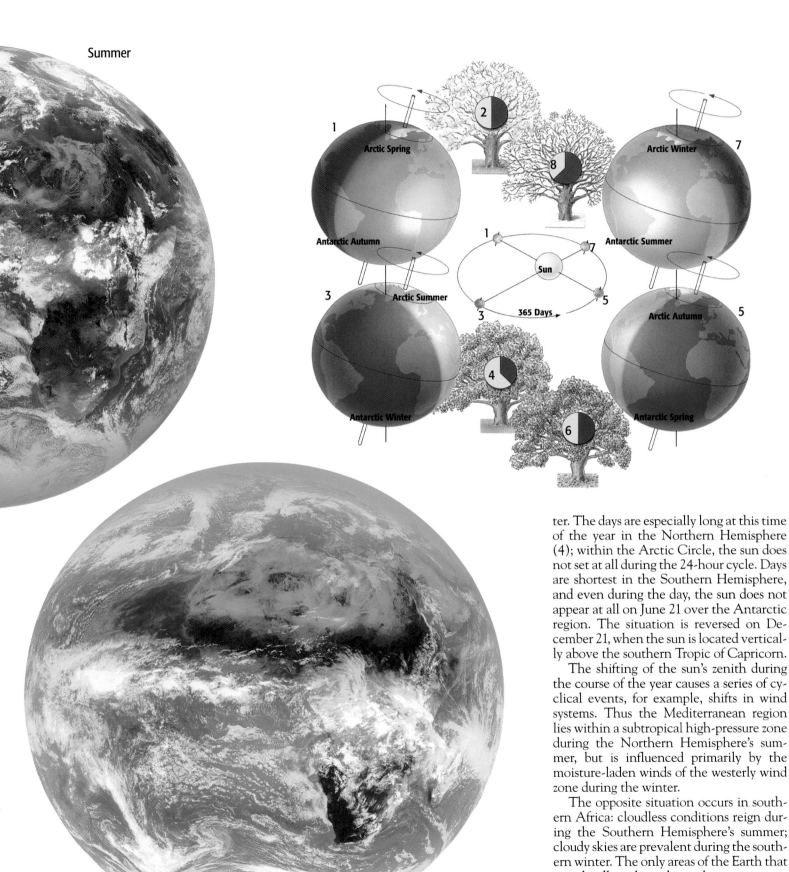

Winter

ter. The days are especially long at this time of the year in the Northern Hemisphere (4); within the Arctic Circle, the sun does not set at all during the 24-hour cycle. Days are shortest in the Southern Hemisphere, and even during the day, the sun does not appear at all on June 21 over the Antarctic region. The situation is reversed on December 21, when the sun is located vertically above the southern Tropic of Capricorn.

The shifting of the sun's zenith during the course of the year causes a series of cyclical events, for example, shifts in wind systems. Thus the Mediterranean region lies within a subtropical high-pressure zone during the Northern Hemisphere's summer, but is influenced primarily by the moisture-laden winds of the westerly wind zone during the winter.

The opposite situation occurs in southern Africa: cloudless conditions reign during the Southern Hemisphere's summer; cloudy skies are prevalent during the southern winter. The only areas of the Earth that are cloudless throughout the year are regions, such as the Sahara and Arabian deserts, and the Namibian desert on the coast of southwest Africa.

# Settlement Patterns and Economic R

**Regions of Human Settlement and
Economic Development,
Depicted According to Sources of Light**

light sources

This nighttime satellite image provides a good depiction of the Earth's population distribution. Numerous closely delimited "bright spots" stand out. These are not solely the sites of the greatest population concentrations, but also oil-production sites where gas is flared off. Some examples of this are the Persian Gulf, oil oases in the Sahara, production sites in southern Nigeria, and the so-called Third Baku in the midst of the

# ions of the Earth

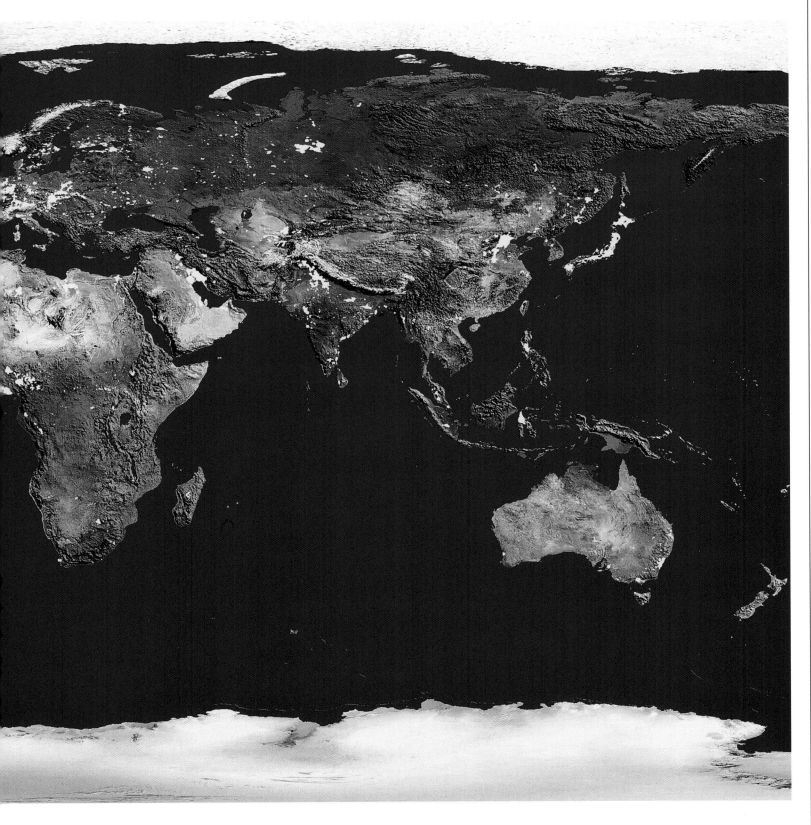

west Siberian lowlands. Areas of widespread population concentration include the Manufacturing Belt in the United States, parts of central and western Europe, the Greater Moscow metropolitan area, the Ganges lowlands, the Great Plain of northern China, and the Japanese archipelago. Heavily populated areas in the Southern Hemisphere include southeastern Australia and certain sites along the Atlantic coast of South America. Human habitation tends to concentrate near the coasts and in lowland areas beside major rivers. The Earth's vast deserts and forested regions are nearly devoid of human habitation.

# The Contours of the Earth

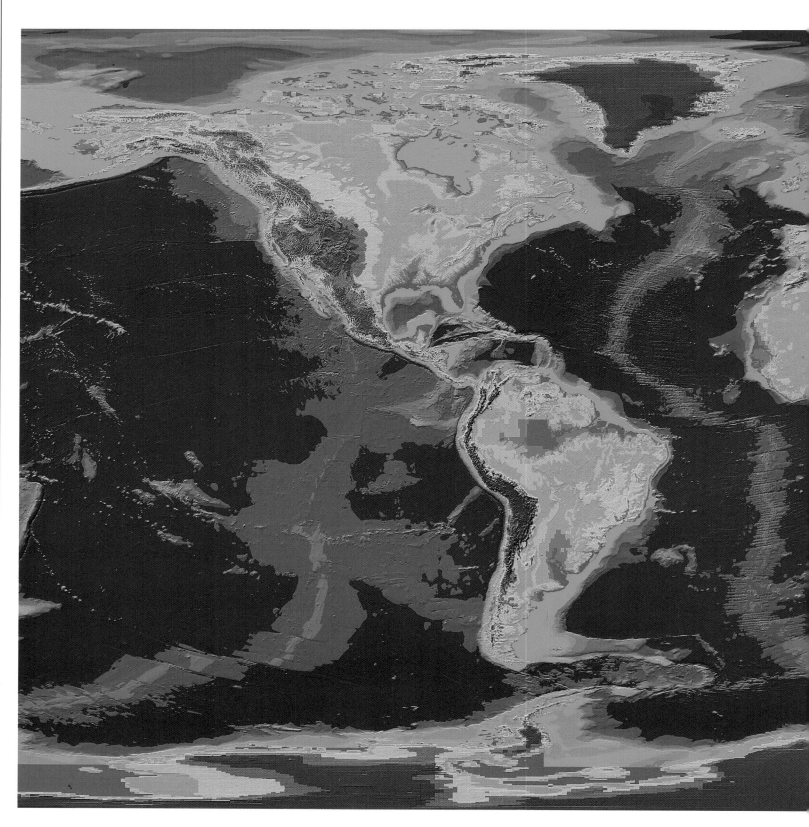

**Depth** (below mean sea level)

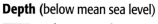 under 20,000 feet

20,000 – 13,000 feet

13,000 – 10,000 feet

10,000 – 6,500 feet

6,500 – 3,300 feet

3,300 – 1,600 feet

1,600 – 650 feet

650 – 0 feet

**Elevation** (above mean sea level)

0 – 3.3 feet

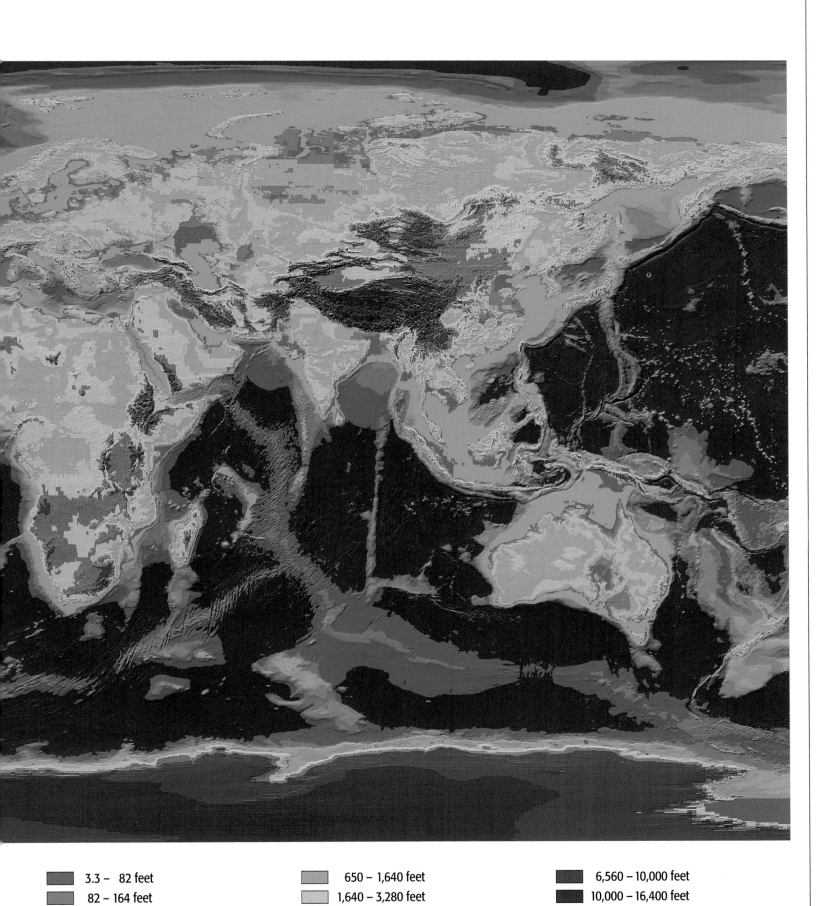

| | | |
|---|---|---|
| 3.3 – 82 feet | 650 – 1,640 feet | 6,560 – 10,000 feet |
| 82 – 164 feet | 1,640 – 3,280 feet | 10,000 – 16,400 feet |
| 164 – 330 feet | 3,280 – 5,000 feet | over 16,400 feet |
| 330 – 660 feet | 5,000 – 6,560 feet | |

# The Contours of the Ocean Floor

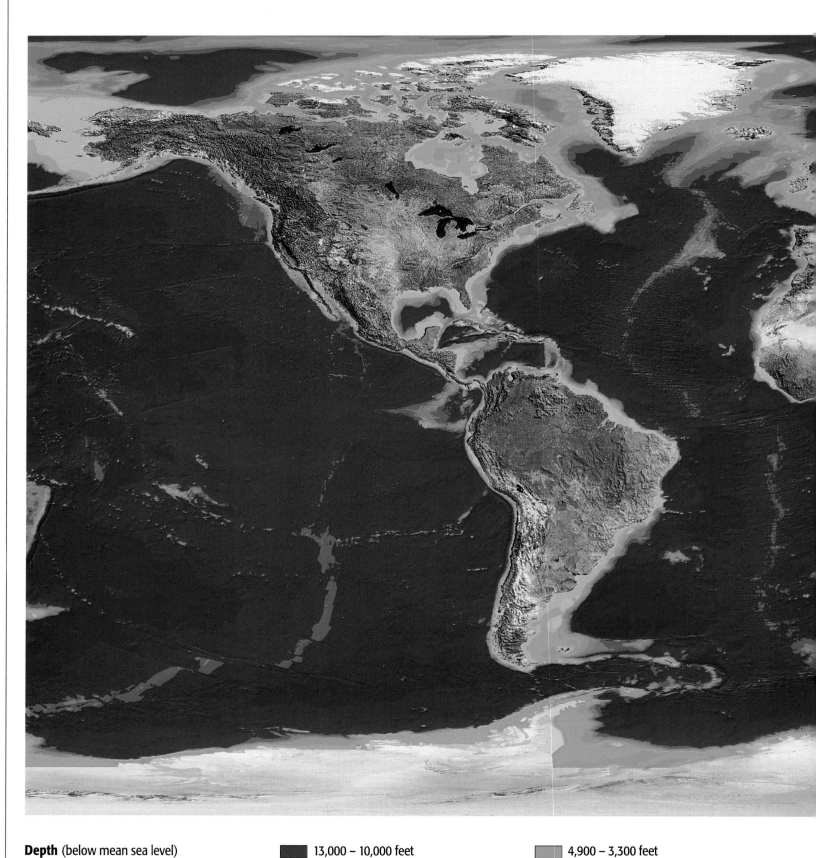

**Depth** (below mean sea level)

| | | |
|---|---|---|
| under 20,000 feet | 13,000 – 10,000 feet | 4,900 – 3,300 feet |
| 20,000 – 16,400 feet | 10,000 – 8,200 feet | 3,300 – 2,500 feet |
| 16,400 – 13,000 feet | 8,200 – 6,500 feet | 2,500 – 1,300 feet |
| | 6,500 – 4,900 feet | 1,300 – 650 feet |

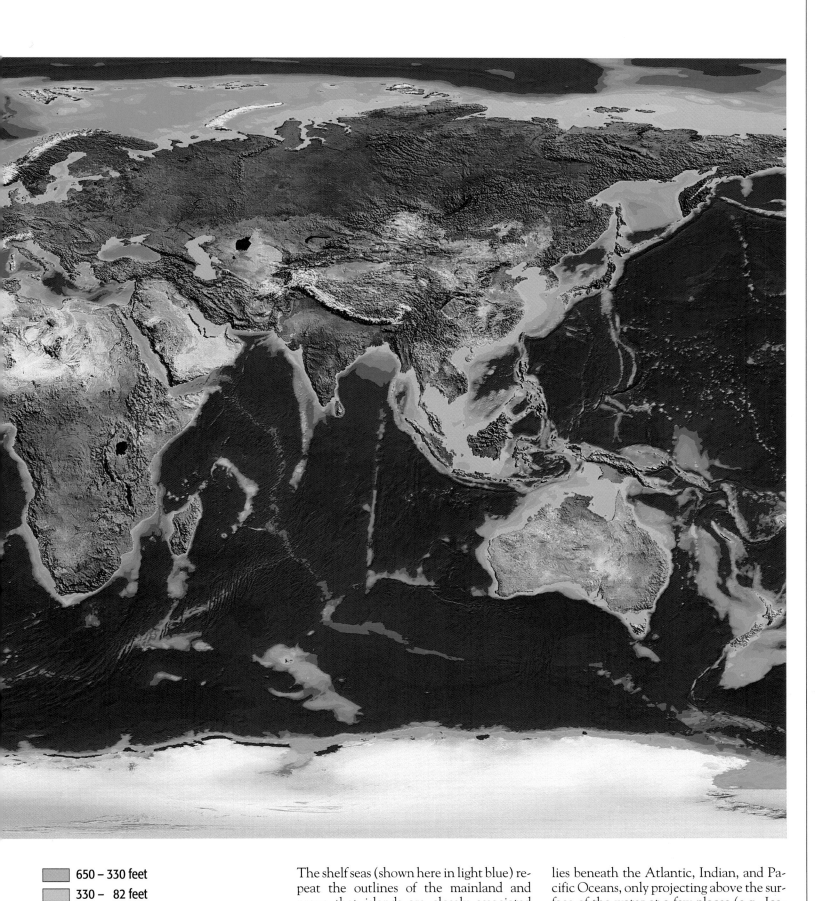

650 – 330 feet
330 – 82 feet
82 – 0 feet

The shelf seas (shown here in light blue) repeat the outlines of the mainland and prove that islands are closely associated with their neighboring continents. The Earth's largest continuous mountain range lies beneath the Atlantic, Indian, and Pacific Oceans, only projecting above the surface of the water at a few places (e.g., Iceland and the Maldive Islands).

# Plate Tectonics

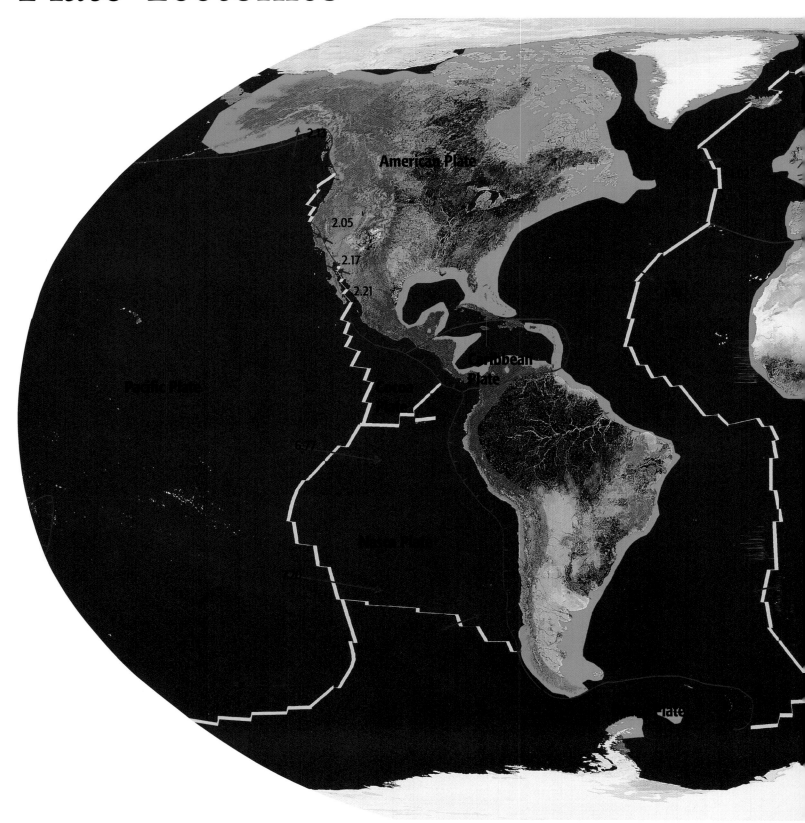

American Plate

2.05

2.17

2.21

Pacific Plate

Caribbean Plate

## Fault Zones and Plate Boundaries

| | | |
|---|---|---|
| ▨ shelf | ▨ fault zones |  hypothetical plate boundaries |
| ▨ alpidic fold zones | ◤ mid-ocean ridges |  2,91 plate drift in inches per year |
| | ■ subduction zones | |
| | ■ other plate boundaries | |

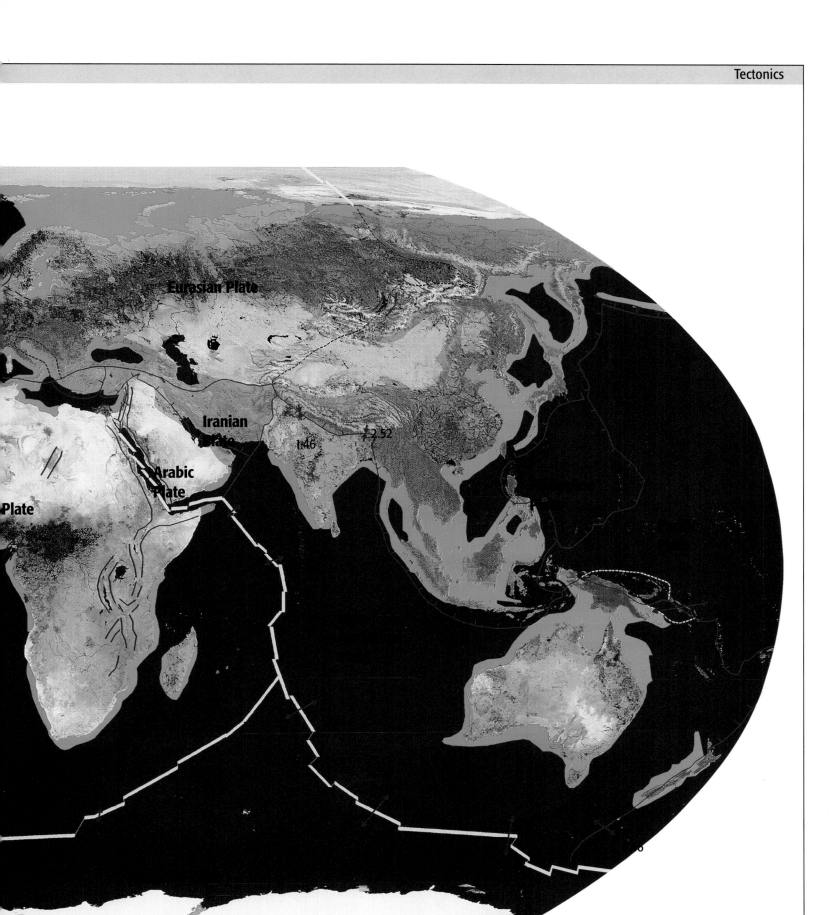

According to the theory of plate tectonics, the crust of the Earth has been broken into numerous slabs, which are moved by currents in the Earth's mantle. Propelled by the ascending and diverging arms of these deep convection currents, the plates drift apart and new crust forms to fill the gap. Currents beneath the crust converge at subduction zones, drawing the oceanic plate under the continental plate. Where plates collide, the crust folds and mountains are raised. Hence, the edges of the plates are the Earth's weakest points; tensions increase in the rocks here, and these tensions are released as earthquakes and volcanic eruptions.

# The San Andreas Fault

Every day as many as five minor tremors shake the Californian Pacific Coast. Cracks and fissures in streets, bridges, and pipes, as well as deformations of railroad tracks, are part of everyday life. More than 47 earthquakes with magnitudes of 6.5 or more on the Richter scale have been recorded in California since the year 1800. The cause of these smaller and larger tremors is the San Andreas Fault, which runs more than 600 miles (1,000 kilometers) through California in a northwesterly direction from the Gulf of California in Mexico to Cape Mendocino in northern California. The primary fault line is visible in the satellite photo, where it extends from the northwestern corner to the eastern edge of the picture.

This natural phenomenon can be explained according to contemporary tectonic theory, which asserts that the Earth's surface is in constant horizontal movement. The Earth's outer shell, which is about 60-miles (100-kilometers) thick, is built from six large solid plates and a number of smaller ones, all of which float atop a semi-fluid, reduced-friction substrate much the way slabs of ice float on water. In the California region, the boundary between the Pacific and North American Plates passes partly beneath the ocean, partly beneath dry land. The Pacific Plate grows from the East Pacific Ridge, presses against the North American Plate, and pushes its way toward the northwest. Meanwhile, the continental plate drifts southeastward alongside the Pacific Plate at a speed that varies between 0.6 inches (1.5 centimeters) and 2.8 inches (7 centimeters) per year.

The San Andreas Fault is actually a complex system consisting of one main fault line and numerous smaller branches, together with a complicated mosaic of crustal fragments. Depending on the direction

of the shift, either basin-forming or folded uplifted structural zones develop. For example, Los Angeles lies within one of these basins. On the other hand, the Santa Lucia and Diabolo Mountains, which are part of the Coast Range, coincide with zones of folding. Recent volcanism and the localized emission of hot liquids are relatively harmless effects caused by ongoing crustal movements.

Irregularities in orientation, in the composition of rocks, and in geothermal conditions along the system's fault lines cause many different kinds of movements. "Creeping" movements occur continually in some segments of the system (mainly in southern California), but can be blocked for many years in the San Francisco and Los Angeles regions. The tensions that have accumulated over these periods of time discharge periodically and suddenly as strong

*Like a gaping wound, the San Andreas Fault forms a clearly visible fissure or longitudinal valley in the Carrizo Plain north of Los Angeles.*

earthquakes, often causing horizontal displacements of up to 39 feet (12 meters). The magnitude of the forces unleashed and of the destruction caused when these "time bombs" explode is evident, for example, in the earthquake of January 17, 1994. That earthquake measured 6.8 on the Richter scale and caused 60 deaths. Damage to property was estimated at between 20 and 30 billion dollars, of which only about 6 billion dollars' worth was covered by insurance. Although everyone is well aware of the probability of an even larger earthquake (the so-called Big One), neither the state nor the people are making full use of every possibility available to protect themselves from disaster. Nowadays, city maps show zones in which fissures are likely to occur, telephone books provide detailed emergency-procedure information, and real estate agents are required by law to inform potential buyers if a piece of property is located in a high-risk area. Most of these zones lie in sparsely populated, mountainous regions, but they also extend into the heavily irrigated agricultural areas of the San Joaquin Valley in the northeastern corner of the photo, where new settlements continue to be built.

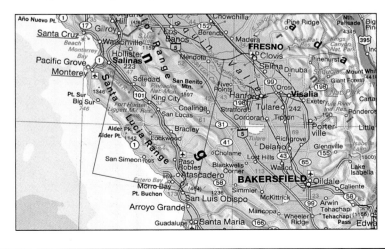

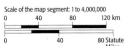

Scale of the map segment: 1 to 4,000,000

# Earthquakes and Volcanism

Tectonic theory hypothesizes that the individual plates of the Earth's crust float on and are moved by viscous currents within the planet's mantle. These plates interlock along their boundaries with one another, creating tensions in the rock there. When these tensions are abruptly released, earthquakes shake the Earth's surface. Volcanic activity also occurs in these crustal zones.

Land areas endangered by earthquakes (but not seaquake-prone areas) are depicted here according to degrees of intensity. Nearly continuous bands of earthquake-prone coastline surround the Pacific and parts of the Indian Ocean. In these subduction zones, oceanic crust dives below the continental crust, where it melts. The active volcanoes of the "Ring of Fire" around the Pacific are indicative of this subduction and melting. Where convection currents diverge, crustal plates drift apart. The separation of the plates is marked by rift valleys within the continents and by volcanoes. The opposite sequence of events occurs at the points where the African and Indian Plates collide with the Eurasian Plate, causing uplift and the formation of folded mountains. Hot spots, whose diameter can vary from 62 to 93 miles (100 to 150 kilometers) are independent of these crustal movements. Hot spots are like chimneys for material rising from the Earth's mantle; crustal plates simply slide across them.

**Degree of Danger Due to Earthquakes**
Maximal degrees of intensity according to the Mercalliscale, with a 20 percent probability of being exceeded within 50 years

- Zone 1: Maximal Intensity VI
- Zone 2: Maximal Intensity VII
- Zone 3: Maximal Intensity VIII
- Zone 4: Maximal Intensity IX or more

**Volcano and Hot Spot Locations**

- ▲ Volcanoes
- ☐ Hot Spots

Volcanism

The primary tremor that shook the Japanese harbor cities of Kobe and Osaka in January 1995 lasted only 20 seconds. With a magnitude of 7.2 on the Richter scale, this earthquake claimed more than 6,000 lives and caused tremendous devastation.

Tinakula Island is one of the Solomon Islands, a part of the Melanesian island group located northeast of Australia in the western Pacific. Tropical rain forest covers the lower slopes of this nearly ideally shaped volcanic cone; cloud forest begins at altitudes above 4,900 feet (1,500 meters).

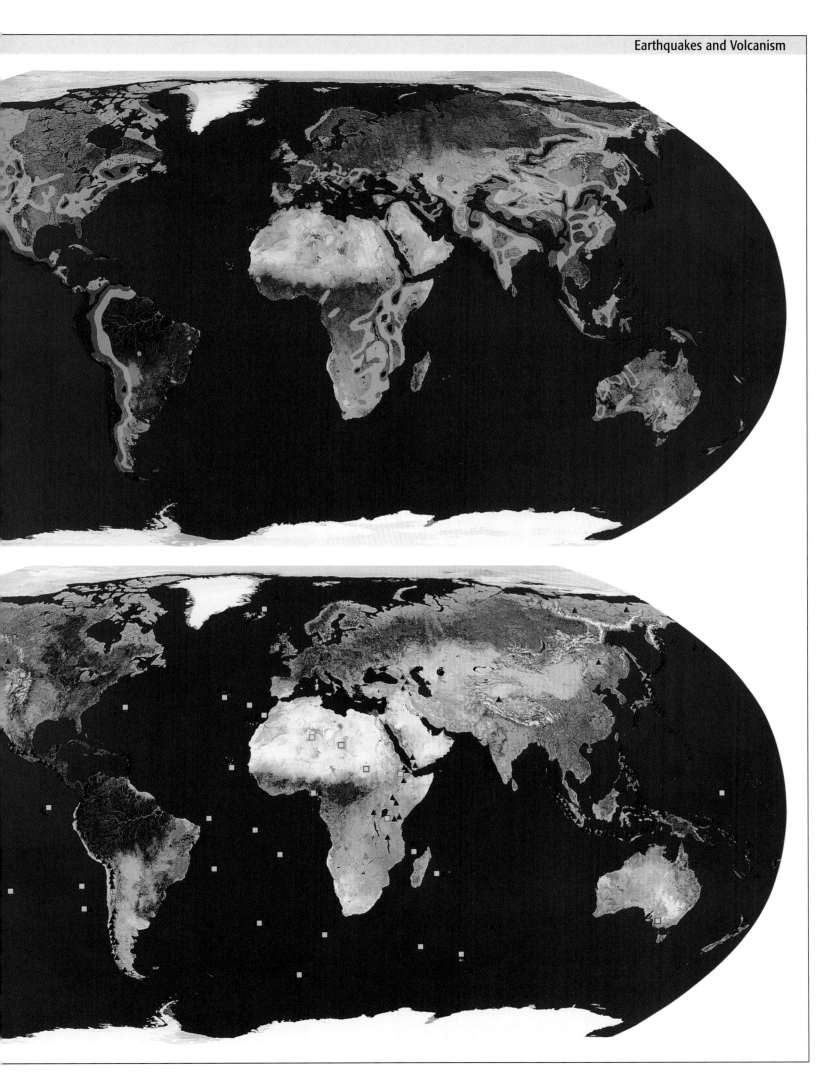

# Mount Saint Helens

*The largest volcanic eruption in North America's recent history took place in May 1980. After having emitted clouds of steam and ashes since March, Mount Saint Helens exploded on May 18, 1980. The blast rained ashes up to a distance of 500 miles (800 kilometers). The energy released by the eruption was equivalent to the explosion of 500 atomic bombs of the type dropped on Hiroshima.*

The barren, desertlike region in the north central portion of the photograph is the region of Mount Saint Helens, with its oval caldera and Spirit Lake. Until May 1980, this 9,678-foot (2,950-meter) mountain with its ice-and-snow-covered summit resembled Mount Hood (11,234 feet = 3,424 meters), at the southeastern corner of the photograph, and Mount Adams (12,306 feet = 3,751 meters), visible to the east of Mount Saint Helens. All three are conical volcanoes with steep slopes and radially oriented streams of lava, deeply fissured and glacially modified. These volcanoes belong to the Cascade Range (along the eastern edge of the photo) in which North America's active volcanoes are arranged in a row stretching from Lassen Peak in northern California to Mount Garibaldi in southern British Columbia. This geologically recent mountain range is located above the site where the Pacific Plate pushes itself beneath the North American Plate. This subduction causes crustal material to melt. The magma rises from a depth of about 60 miles (ca. 100 kilometers) and collects in magma chambers at depths ranging from 6 to 12 miles (10 to 20 kilometers). Cooling and crystallization cause gases to form. The explosive eruption of these gases creates a chimney through which ashes, lapilli, volcanic bombs, and lava ascend.

After a hiatus of more than a century, Mount Saint Helens again became active in 1980. This volcano's most recent previous eruption had been in 1857. Tremors began shaking the area in March 1980. A bulge formed on the north side of the mountain. On May 18, the volcano exploded and lost 1,312 feet (400 meters) of elevation. A rapidly rising cloud of ashes caused thunderstorms; snow and glacial ice melted; and Spirit Lake overflowed. A 33-foot (10-meter) = high torrent of mud rolled toward the valley at a speed of about 50 miles (80 kilometers) per hour and poured into the Columbia River, which breaks through the Cascade Range in a gigantic canyon. Tree trunks and mud blocked ship passage there for several days.

A cloud hot of gases issued from a rent in the northern flank of the mountain, incinerating all the trees within a radius of 1,000 feet (300 meters), uprooting and snapping others as far as 19 miles (30 kilometers) away. Sixty people were killed by this cloud of gas.

Today, we can see the scars left by the eruption. Streams of lava, mud, and debris stretch into the surrounding area. These same phenomena are found on Mount Adams and Mount Hood, although they are less noticeable there because they are partly covered by overgrown vegetation or hidden beneath masses of ice.

In addition to the elongated artificial lakes, other tourist attractions of the Cascade Range's recreation areas are the region's luxuriant forests with their Douglas firs. Their verdure is interrupted by paler

Scale of the map segment: 1 to 4,000,000

0    40    80    120    160    200 km

0    40    80    120    160 Statute Miles

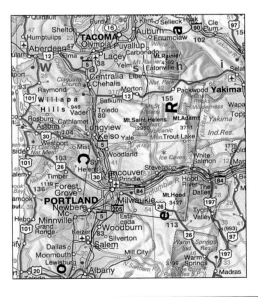

# Hot Spots on Hawaii

The Hawaiian Archipelago stretches 1,500 miles (2,400 kilometers) across the central Pacific Ocean. With the exception of a few atolls, the eight principal islands and more than 120 smaller islands represent the peaks of a colossal chain of volcanoes. The volcanoes Mauna Loa (13,681 feet = 4,170 meters) and Mauna Kea (13,796 feet = 4,205 meters) are among the Earth's highest mountains, rising more than 29,500 feet (9,000 meters) from the ocean floor, which lies almost 16,400 feet = 5,000 meters below sea level.

The volcanoes of the Hawaiian Islands may have been created by a source of magma believed to originate deep within the Earth's mantle. The alignment of the islands – like pearls on a string – is explained by the theory of plate tectonics. Kauai, the most northwesterly island in the group, is also the oldest of these islands with an age of 5.6 million years. Hawaii, in the southeast, is the largest and youngest in the chain; its origins lie a "mere" half-million years in the past. In other areas of the Earth, weak zones in the Earth's crust caused by

Scientists have no doubt that the volcanoes that created the Hawaiian Islands broke through the Earth's surface, one after another, in a straight line running from the northwest to the southeast. Beneath the ocean southeast of Hawaii, the next volcano is already beginning to build its future island.

The satellite photograph shows the volcanoes Haleakala (on Maui), Mauna Kea, and Mauna Loa (on Hawaii); only the last is still active today. One indication of this activity is the presence of dark streams of barren lava extending from its crater. Mauna Loa's most recent major eruptions occurred in 1975 and 1984. Just beyond the edge of the photograph lies 4,078-foot (1,243-meter) Kilauea, with a constantly simmering sea of lava inside its crater.

Haleakala Crater (10,020 feet = 3,054 meters) on Maui is one of the Earth's largest. It is 20 miles (32 kilometers) in circumference and 1,970 feet (600 meters) deep.

Both of the islands in the satellite photograph show obvious differences in the types of vegetation found on their north-

east and southwest sides. The northeastern slope is clad in intense green, while the southwestern face displays brownish to yellowish tones. The northeast trade winds, cooled by the Pacific, ventilate this group of islands. Their windward sides therefore receive abundant precipitation of as much as 47 inches (1,200 millimeters) per year. Lush mountain forests thrive there up to elevations of 6,600 to 7,550 feet (2,000 to 2,300 meters). In contrast, the volcanoes' lee sides lie within a "rain shadow": because they receive only about 24 inches (600 mm) of annual precipitation, they are clad with a much sparser covering of vegetation. Highly mechanized, coastal plantations primarily grow sugarcane and pineapple, augmented by less extensive cultivation of bananas, vegetables, and coffee; drier areas are devoted to extensive grasslands for the grazing of cattle. Tourism, which attracts some eight million each year, is extremely important to the economy of the entire region.

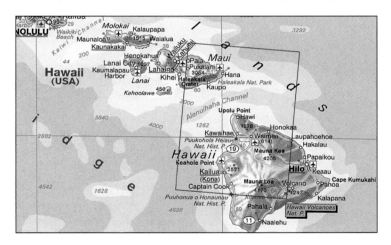

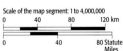

Scale of the map segment: 1 to 4,000,000

the collision or drifting apart of gigantic crustal plates are responsible for volcanic eruptions. The Hawaiian Islands, on the other hand, are located far away from the nearest subduction or collision zones.

Only tectonic theory can offer a reasonable explanation for the "splendid isolation" of Hawaii's mighty volcanoes. According to this theory, the Pacific Plate is slowly drifting toward the northwest. As it progresses, it slides across a super-heated, stationary stream of material called a hot spot. Volcanoes erupt directly above the hot spot; their activity subsides and finally ends altogether when the eruption site on the plate has slid far enough away from the underlying hot spot.

*The temperature of the lava exceeds 1,800° Fahrenheit (1,000° Celsius) when it emerges from Kilauea Crater and begins to flow toward the valley. Kilauea is about 28 miles (45 kilometers) from Mauna Loa, which is considerably larger. The island's indigenous residents call the nearly circular crater with its constantly simmering sea of lava "Halemaumau," (heart of the eternal fire).*

# Atmospheric Circulation

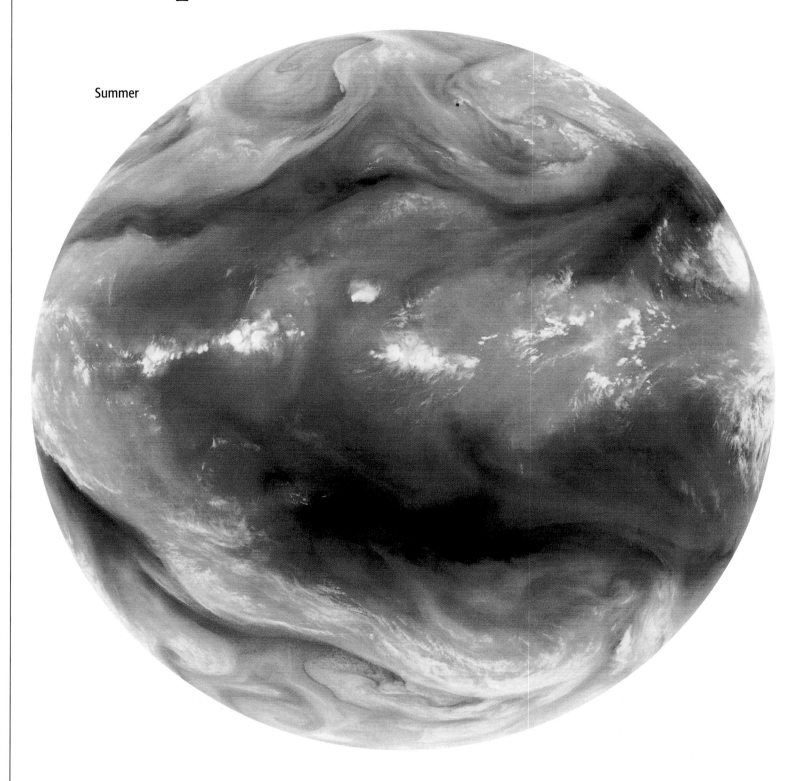

Summer

"Parked" at a height of 22,400 miles (36,000 kilometers) in geostationary orbit above the Equator, the Meteosat 2 satellite produces photos in the visible-light, infrared, and water-vapor spectral ranges at 30-minute intervals. Its sensors detect radiation reflected by atmospheric water vapor, creating images that make visible the worldwide processes of exchange taking place in our planet's airy envelope. Paler areas indicate moister regions; darker colors represent drier areas.

The photo above provides a nearly ideally typical view of atmospheric circulation. In the middle, near the Equator, warm air rises to great heights. This area is considered to be calm, since rising or falling air is not perceived by human beings as wind. The northeast and southeast trade winds meet here, creating towering thunderheads in the subtropical convergence zone. At the latitudes of the tropics, the air descends again and the clouds disperse. The dark shades in this part of the photo represent

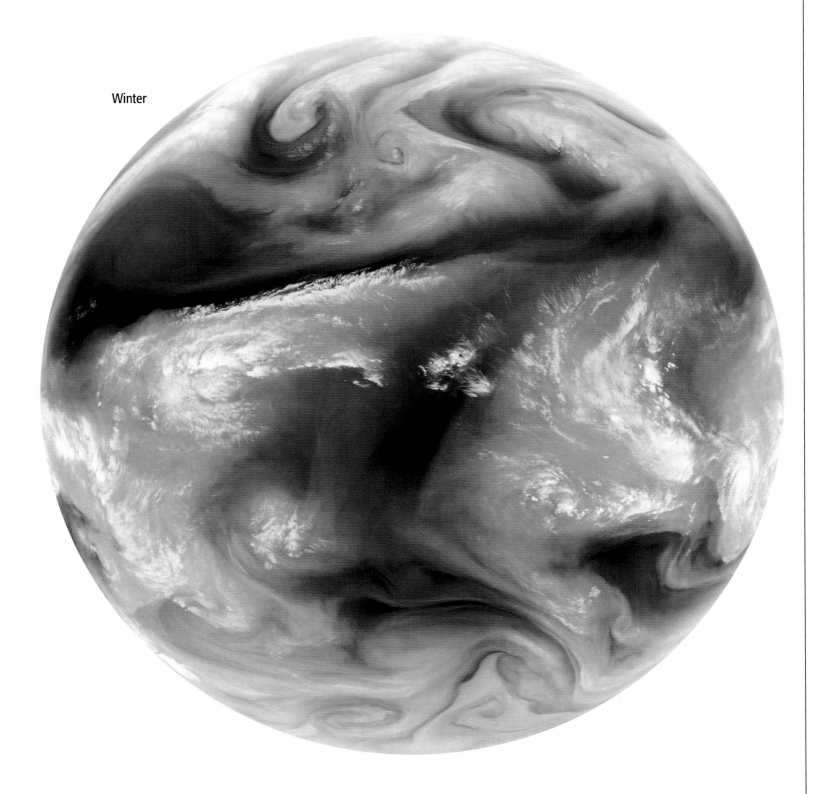

Winter

the low humidity of this high-pressure belt. Closer to the ground, the trade winds stream out of this area and toward equatorial low-pressure troughs, where they converge. The spiraling cloud systems of the cyclones appear in the middle latitudes closer to the poles. Especially in these latitudes in the Southern Hemisphere, prevailing westerly winds blow with great regularity and constancy to create the so-called Roaring Forties.

A similar pattern of atmospheric circulation is also evident in the photo above, although here the swirling individual "systems" are more complexly interwoven. This interweaving is caused in part by the unequal distribution of the Earth's landmasses and oceans, in part by the location and extent of high-altitude mountain ranges. Both of these factors influence the Earth's wind systems.

# The Expansion of the Deserts

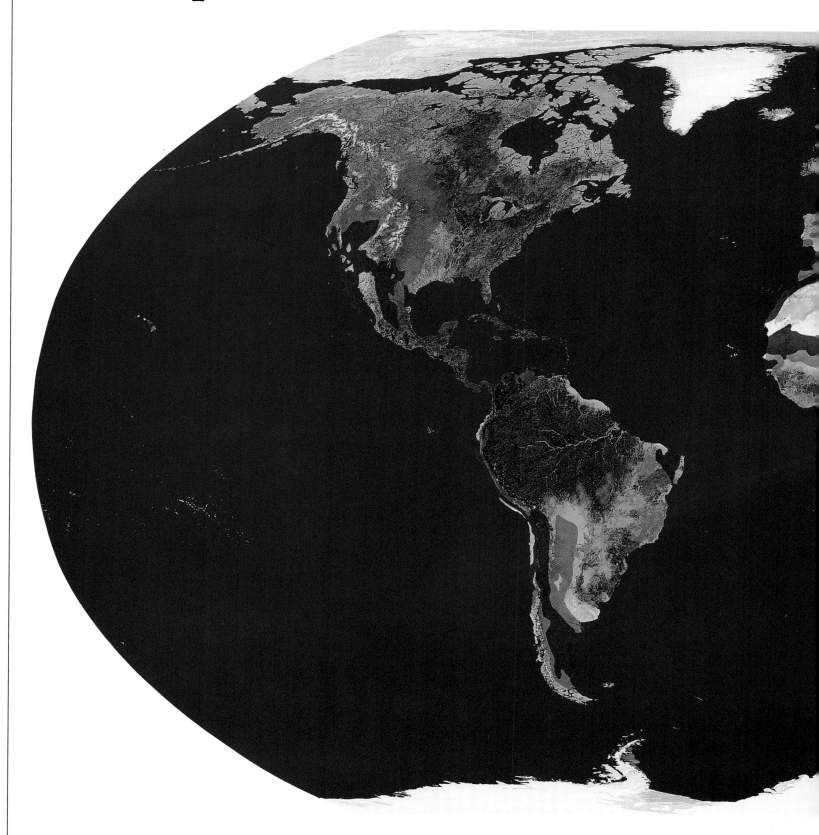

## The Threat of Desertification

- ⬛ severely endangered
- ⬜ less severely jeopardized

Desertification – the expansion of the deserts – is one of the gravest problems facing the Earth today. The satellite photo map of the world shows the regions endangered by the advance of the deserts. The causes of the inexorable growth of the deserts lie in natural long-term variations in the weather, climatic destabilization, human intervention in the environment due to overpopulation and economic changes, or in

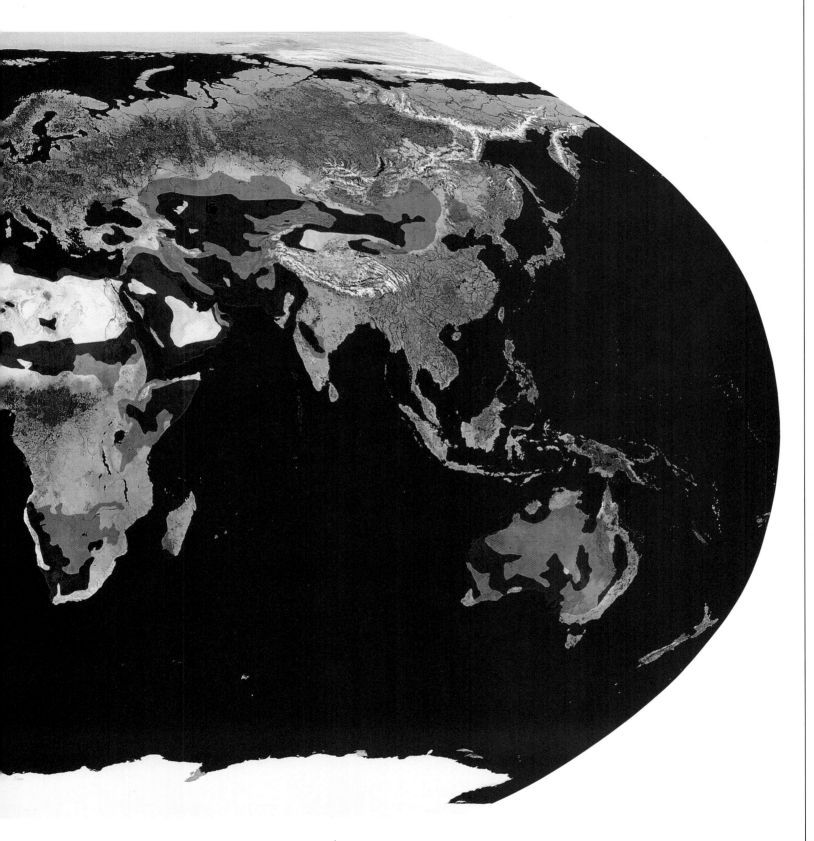

combinations of these contributing factors. Large-scale synoptic views taken over extended periods of time are needed in order to better understand these processes, investigate their causes, and comprehend their effects on the Earth's overall ecological system. Satellite photographs offer us precisely this vantage point. They show movements in vegetation zones and habitat boundaries over the course of seasons and years, and enable us to discern the sequence of these changes in a holistic fashion. They also shed light on the ways in which human beings react to ecological changes.

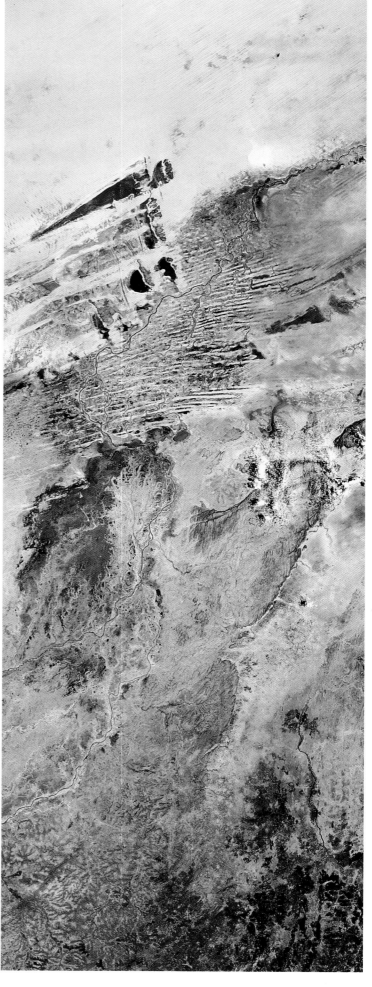

# The Sahel Zone: A Threatened Habitat

The ecosystems of the transitional areas between various climatic regions, and especially those that lie between the Earth's vast desert belts and their adjacent semiarid and subhumid regions, are particularly threatened by the global changes currently taking place.

Under the influence of human actions and reactions to natural, cyclical variations or to global environmental changes, conditions in these sensitive regions are changing at an accelerating rate.

Increased population pressure with its constantly growing needs for habitat, food-

during dry spells or water erosion after heavy rains are the chief causes of environmental degradation in this region.

Along with the annual cycles of dry and rainy seasons, long-lasting droughts are cyclical phenomena that periodically recur at multiyear intervals.

Data regularly relayed to Earth by the European weather satellite Meteosat, which hovers in a geostationary "parking" orbit 21,000 miles (36,000 kilometers) above the Sahel Zone, show daily and annual patterns of cloud cover as well as the frequency of storms and percipitation.

Throughout the course of each year, the tropical cloud belt that girds the planet shifts from south to north in response to the sun's apparent movement. This shift determines the timing of annual rainy and dry seasons.

High-resolution satellite photos help determine the precipitation situation and calculate the so-called vegetation index, which quantifies ongoing changes in plant cover. Only the highest-resolution photos (like those shown here) taken by the camera system aboard the American Landsat satellite offer detailed insights about actual conditions on the ground. When compared over several years' time, these images depict the vicious circle of events in the Sahel Zone. The predicament is especially obvious when one views satellite photos taken of extensive areas at different seasons of the year and over the course of many years. During the 17-year period spanned by these photos, the arid region has expanded some 120 miles (200 kilometers) southward. Pages 38 and 40 present four such satellite photos showing a cross-section of the transitional region extending from tropical hill country in the south to the full desert of the Sahara in the north. Between these two extremes lie areas of semidesert and desert steppe traversed from south to north by the Niger River's inland delta.

The first pair of photos (p. 38) depicts the status of vegetation during the dry season in 1974 (left) and 1989; the second pair (p. 40) shows its status during the rainy seasons of those same years. These images

stuffs and water is gravely aggravating the problems already facing these ecosystems and leading to long-lasting, widespread deterioration of entire landscapes. Satellite photos make the problem visible, clearly revealing how a given habitat can change for the better or for the worse.

Observations made over a medium-long period of time, together with comparisons of photographs taken at an interval of 17 years, show that the desert in the Sahel Zone, whose 1.1 million square miles (3.1 million square kilometers) account for approximately 10 percent of Africa's surface area, is expanding southward.

Water shortage, deforestation, and destruction of plant cover through overgrazing, followed by wind erosion of the soil

*Along the Niger near Mopti, the regional capital, during the dry season. Favored by lack of vegetation, the wind encounters few obstacles and fills the air with yellowish particles of sand.*

*The city is located on three islands on the floodplain at the junction of the Niger and Bani Rivers.*

Scale of the map segment: 1 to 12,000,000

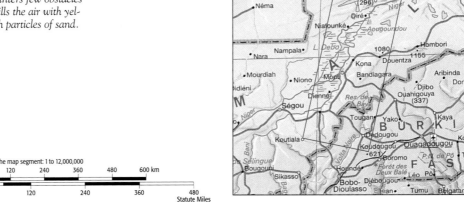

have been altered as infrared, false-color photos; reddish tones represent vegetation. This shade provides a clear contrast with plant-free zones, which appear as yellow or brownish areas, and also shows more obvious gradations of color within itself so that the observer can distinguish between areas where plant cover is denser or sparser.

If one looks closely at these photos, several zones can be distinguished along a north-south axis. These begin with the bright yellow shades of the full desert, which gradually changes into the sparse vegetation of thorn savanna or arid savanna. The boundaries of this ecosystem are difficult to locate because they merge almost imperceptibly into grassland, which the infrared satellite photo depicts as an area of reddish tones. Depending on the status of the vegetation and the amount of moisture, this area can appear as a rich, reddish tone.

These photos show one part of a region where long-lasting dry periods have caused

the tragedies that have been so widely reported by the world's news media.

The amount of annual precipitation in this region increases from 8 inches (200 millimeters) in the north to 23 inches (600 millimeters) in the south; annual variations of 25 percent are common. The 8-inch (200-millimeter) isohyet is the lowest limit beneath which nonirrigated agriculture becomes impossible. This line forms the northern border of the Sahel Zone. In the south, the Sahel is bounded by the 27-inch (700-millimeter) isohyet, where the habitat changes into a region characterized by Sudanese-type vegetation.

In short and long cycles lasting from 2 to 3, 7 to 11, and 28 to 30 years, the Sahel Zone experiences dry spells that lead to the well-known problems. Dry periods that last several years and during which precipitation may decline by as much as 20 percent reduce harvests by up to 25 percent. The growing season for the vegetation, which depends on the precipitation, varies be-

tween 90 and 110 days. Different types of grain require different amounts of water: Italian millet can grow with as little as 8 inches (200 millimeters) of rainfall; sorghum millet in sandy soil yields the best harvests when 18 to 20 inches (450 to 500 millimeters) of rain fall; peanuts need at least 15 inches (380 millimeters) of rain.

The intensity of the vegetation's (red) color mirrors the variations in precipitation conditions. The rains begin four to six weeks after the sun has passed its highest annual elevation. Rain falls between May and October, but only during the months of July and August does precipitation exceed evaporation. The dry season lasts from November through April. The intensive color of the vegetation clearly shows the location of the Niger's inland delta. This "densely cultivated" island owes its life to "foreign water," which rains on the tropical mountainous and hilly regions to the south during the rainy season and is borne northward into the region by the Niger River as much as two months later. This water first fills up the swampy lowlands of the inland delta, then moistens the Paleolithic dune landscape that adjoins the delta to the north, before the excess flows down the Niger River Valley. In the dry season, vegetation is restricted to the deepest sites within the basin.

Some 43 million people inhabit the Sahel Zone, which stretches across Africa. The rate of population growth measures between 2.5 and 3.5 percent.

The region's incessantly growing population depends on agriculture and animal husbandry for its survival. During the dry season, humans and animals alike require a far larger habitat.

Depending on the vegetation density, the amount of pastureland needed to support one cow can vary from 9.3 to 40.75 acres. Severe overgrazing occurs during the dry season, and this, in turn, creates the aforementioned vicious circle. Seasonal migration into greener, more southerly pastures exacerbates the pressure of use on that landscape and starts the desertification process there. This process is apparent when one compares the adjacent photographs in each pair: settlements with their fields and pastures appear as small, pale areas and as branching patterns within the "red" vegetation zones. These changes in the vegetation zones are most readily visible in photos taken during the dry season (p. 38).

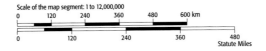

When its waters are high, the Niger River with its main and side arms forms a gigantic inland delta measuring some 40,000 square kilometers in area. Rice is grown in its fertile mud; millet is sown after the water recedes.

Scale of the map segment: 1 to 12,000,000

0    120    240    360    480    600 km

0    120    240    360    480
Statute Miles

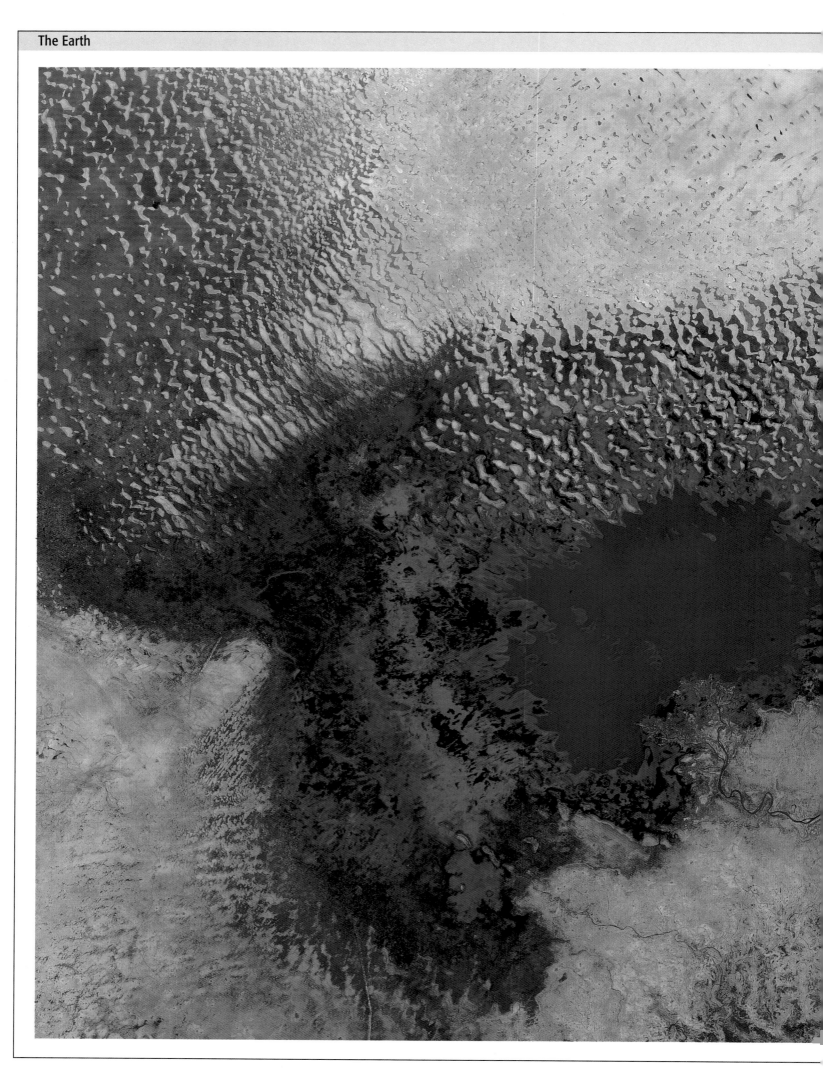

# The Silting Up of Lake Chad

*A dense growth of amphibious vegetation thrives near the shores of Lake Chad and in its tributaries, the Logone and Chari Rivers. These swampy thickets are inhabited by a vast diversity of birds, including crowned cranes, herons, and cormorants, and even provide a home for the only herd of elephants living outside savanna.*

Because its water level changes annually and over longer periods, and because of the drastic variations in its surface, Lake Chad in the Sahel Zone has long been veiled in unsolved mysteries. Although it has no outlet, the lake is nonetheless filled with freshwater. It has a maximum depth of 23 feet (7 meters) and its water volume varies between 388 billion and 1.45 trillion cubic feet (11 and 41 cubic kilometers). With a potential evaporation of more than 1.3 inches (330 millimeters) per year, the existence of the lake is 98 percent dependent upon seasonal precipitation in the moist savannas in the upper watersheds of its tributary Logone-Chari River system.

The "Southern Lake" is visible in the center of the satellite photo. The northwestern corner shows the remnants of the "Northern Lake." Because it receives less water from the Chari, this part of Lake Chad generally dries up first. The Chari's inland delta is clearly visible: this river deposits sediments and mud into the sea from the south. From the northeast (the direction of the nearly incessant trade wind), series of dunes made of Saharan sand march toward the lake and create a diverse amphibious landscape where broad zones of papyrus alternate with sandy islands and clay planes. The encroaching sand has divided the once intact lake into two larger and many smaller individual lakes. Only seldom (most recently in 1963) does the lake swell to its original area of some 9,600 square miles (25,000 square kilometers).

The silting up of the lake is accelerated by the desiccation of the Sahel Zone. This allows formerly stable dunes to become mobile. Furthermore, diversion of irrigation water from the Logone-Chari system reduces the volume of water reaching the lake. For many years, scientists have attempted to correlate changes in the level of Lake Chad with climatic changes and desertification processes in the Sahel Zone.

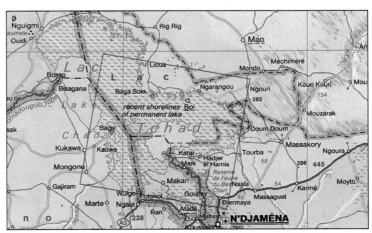

Scale of the map segment: 1 to 4,000,000

0    40    80    120 km

0    40    80 Statute Miles

# The Distribution of the Clouds

The amount of solar radiation depends on day length, which in turn is determined by the position of the sun and the amount of cloud cover. The annual shifting of temperature and climatic zones can be seen in this comparison of the situations that prevail during summer and winter.

The Earth's deserts, especially the arid belt in the Old World, which stretches from the Arabian Desert to central Asia, are the areas receiving the most sunshine. During the summer, the Mediterranean region and Asia Minor are included within this part of the subtropical high-pressure belt. By comparison, the deserts in western North America and the arid regions of the Southern Hemisphere occupy only a relatively small space. The monsoon regions of southern and southeastern Asia are striking. During the period of summer monsoon rains, the sun only seldom manages to pierce the thick cloud cover; during the winter, on the other hand, these countries receive intensive sunlight.

**Average Monthly Length of Sunshine under 1 percent**

- under 1 percent
- 1 – 10 percent
- 10 – 20 percent
- 20 – 30 percent
- 30 – 40 percent
- 40 – 50 percent
- 50 – 60 percent
- 60 – 70 percent
- 70 – 80 percent
- 80 – 90 percent
- 90 – 100 percent

*This photo was taken during an annular eclipse of the sun, when the tip of the moon's umbra no longer extends quite far enough to reach the Earth's surface.*

*The "diamond ring" effect occurs when the sun's rays shine through a lunar valley. The arcing protuberances are ejected from the sun's chromosphere.*

Summer

Winter

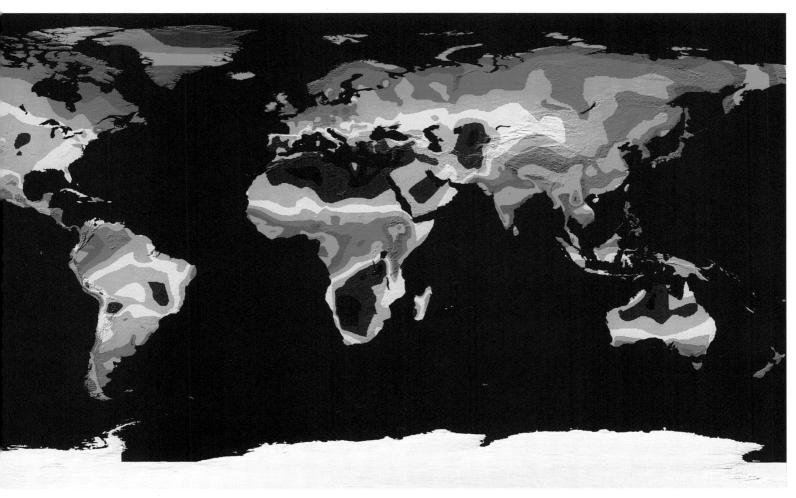

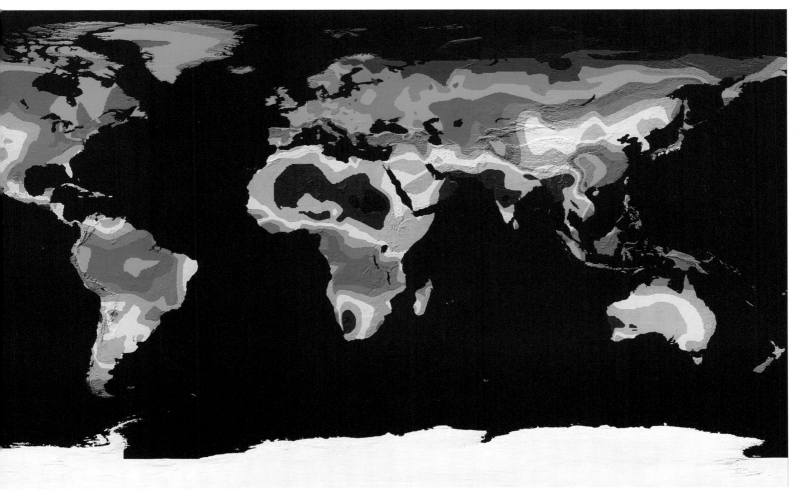

# Hurricane Andrew over Florida

With wind speeds of more than 170 miles per hour (270 kilometers per hour), Hurricane Andrew carved a corridor of devastation through densely settled southern Florida on August 24, 1992, destroying property worth an estimated 24 billion dollars. Forty-seven people were killed; approximately 350,000 were left homeless.

The genesis of tropical cyclones in the Atlantic region can be explained as follows: hot, dry air above the Sahara collides with colder, moister air from the Sahel Zone. This collision spawns small low-pressure waves that drift out over the Atlantic. These waves create short-lived clouds that soon dissipate. But if the water temperature is warmer than 80 degrees Fahrenheit (27 degrees Celsius) and these low-pressure waves drift more than five degrees from the Equator, the Coriolis force sets them into rotary motion. The low-pressure cell rotates counterclockwise toward its center, where pressure is lowest. Hot, moist air over the water's surface rises and is drawn into the rotary motion of the low-pressure system. This air loses moisture through condensation, and the resultant heat of condensation fuels the rotary motor. Firmly embedded within the trade winds, the whirling low-pressure systems continue westwards growing in strength to become full-fledged hurricanes. Most of them turn northward when they reach the western part of the Atlantic. Their speed of progress increases over the warm waters of the Gulf Stream, but they quickly dissipate over colder waters beginning around 35 degrees North latitude. Hurricanes also dissipate quickly when they begin to move across landmasses because they lack fresh supplies of warm, humid air. Sometimes a westerly current, caused by El Niño (see pp. 80–81), stops them.

The satellite photo of August 24, 1992, allows us to peer downward from above

*Hurricane Andrew was especially violent over southern Florida. Almost no buildings were spared in Homestead or in Cutler Ridge (shown in photo). The cyclone created as much bulky trash as was normally generated there in 30 years' time. Partly responsible for the magnitude of the devastation is the flimsy, light style in which many American homes are built.*

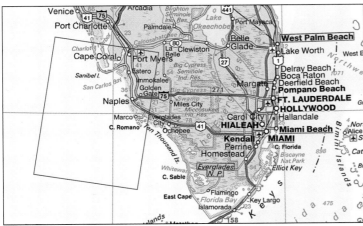

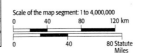

Scale of the map segment: 1 to 4,000,000

| 0 | 40 | 80 | 120 km |

| 0 | 40 | 80 Statute Miles |

into the eye of hurricane Andrew. Its axis of rotation is like a pipe 7 to 44 miles (18 to 70 kilometers) in diameter. Cooling air sinks down the eye and dissipates the clouds; around the eye, warm, moisture-saturated air rises and moves counterclockwise.

The frequency of tropical cyclones has distinctly increased in recent years. Meteorologists believe that this increase could be associated with global warming, which supplies more energy to whirling low-pressure systems.

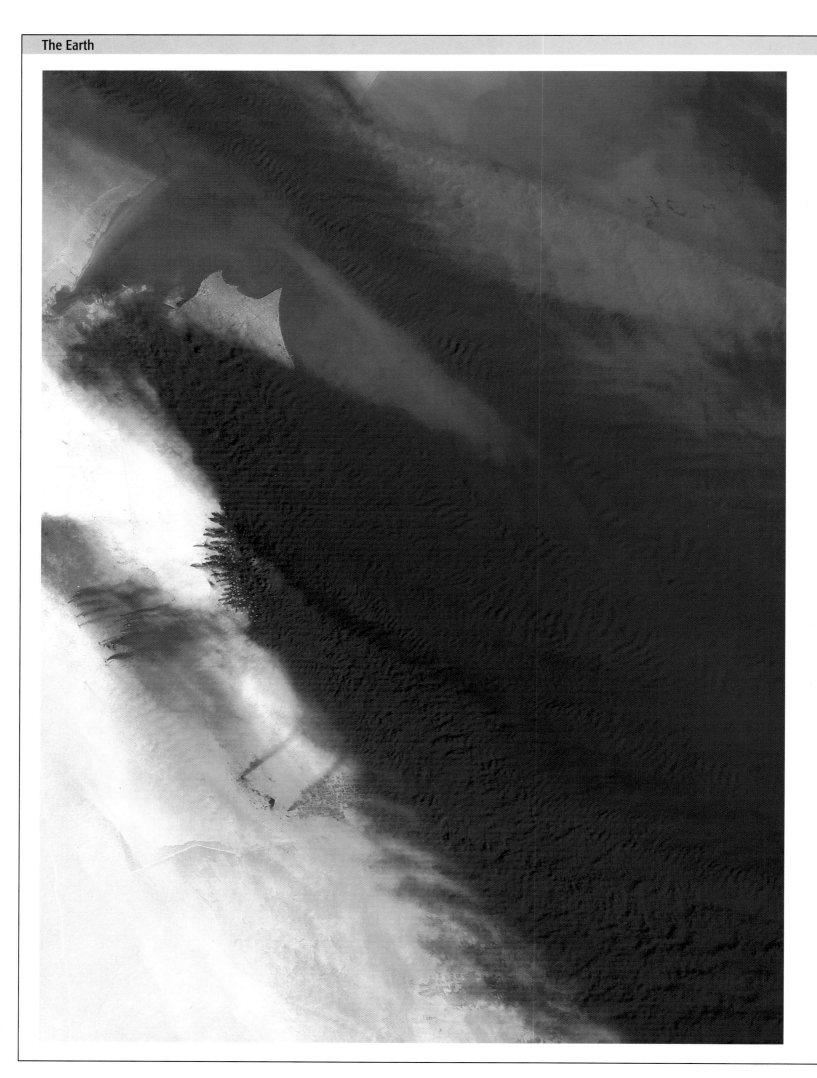

# War for Oil

Dense clouds of smoke rising above burning oil wells obscure the view of the coastline at the northwestern corner of the Arabian-Persian Gulf. Only a few details are visible, for example, the Bay of Kuwait with the small, low-lying islands and harbor installations just offshore from the capital city, al-Kuwait; the al-Wafra oilfield with its pipelines leading to export harbors; and the sand-clay desert steppe of Dibdiba, flat and nearly devoid of vegetation, which gradually descends to meet the shallow shelf sea of the Arabian-Persian Gulf. Only at the northern edge of the Bay of Kuwait is a steep, step-like drop-off discernible.

The desert nation of Kuwait has produced crude oil since 1946, and since then the emirate has developed into one of the world's most important oil-exporting countries. The formerly insignificant harbor town of al-Kuwait became a modern city; the nation's population increased sharply due to immigration; and Kuwait's levels of prosperity and urbanization put it among the world's leaders. It's not surprising that Iraq claimed sovereignty over Kuwaiti territory soon after the latter was granted independence in 1961. On August 2, 1990, Iraq's military attacked its oil-rich neighbor, occupied the country, and declared Kuwait as Iraq's nineteenth province.

To liberate Kuwait, allied forces launched "Operation Desert Storm" on January 17, 1991. To prevent American marines from landing, to shut down seawater desalinization facilities, and to interfere with oil refineries' supplies of cooling water, Iraq deliberately began diverting crude oil into the Gulf on January 23, 1991. Winds caused the oil slick to spread southward along the Kuwaiti and Saudi Arabian coastlines; oily mud washed ashore.

When allied troops forced the Iraqi military to withdraw, the retreating invaders set fire to 727 oil wells. It took 27 teams of firefighters from 11 countries until November 1991 to extinguish the last of those fires. While the fires burned, some eleven thousand tons of soot were released into the atmosphere daily. It was feared that reduction in incident sunshine would lead to widespread cooling as an ecological consequence. Fortunately, the effects remained relatively limited because winds from the northwest, west, and north prevented most of the pollution from contaminating the atmosphere above 6,500 feet (2,000 meters).

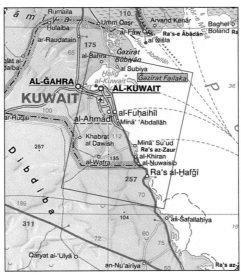

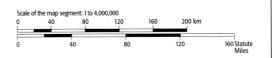

In the middle of this picture, which was taken one year after the Gulf War, the contrasts are clearly visible between the soot-particle-covered, "burned," desert soil and the oil wells, pipeline, and transportation routes of Burgan, one of the world's largest oilfields. The appearance of the coastline is largely influenced by harbors, refineries, and industrial sites, especially al-Kuwait, where croplands are irrigated with desalinated seawater.

# The Distribution of Precipitation

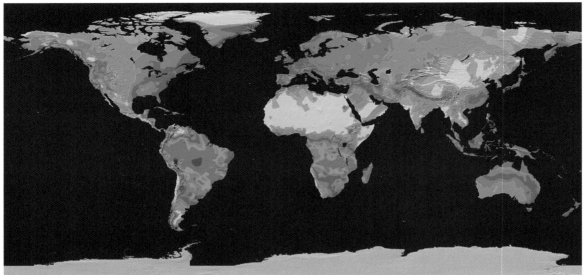
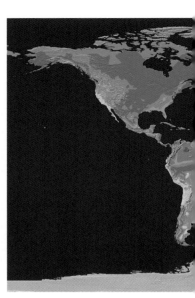

Average amounts of precipitation per month: January

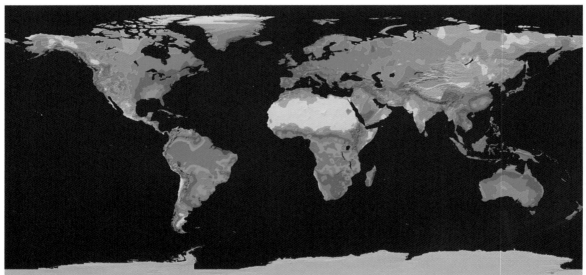

Average amounts of precipitation per month: March

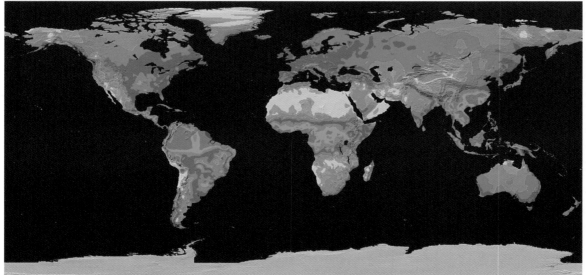

Average amounts of precipitation per month: May

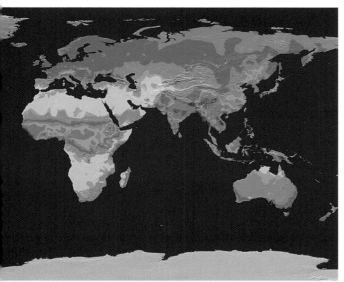

Average amounts of precipitation per month: July

## Average Amounts of Precipitation per Month

- 0.0 – 0.2 inches
- 0.2 – 0.4 inches
- 0.4 – 1.0 inches
- 1.0 – 2.0 inches
- 2.0 – 3.9 inches
- 3.9 – 5.9 inches
- 5.9 – 7.9 inches
- 7.9 – 16 inches
- 16 – 24 inches
- 24 – 40 inches
- more than 40 inches

The distribution of precipitation on the continents of the Earth reflects the dynamics of atmospheric processes throughout the course of the year. The supply of radiant energy varies as the sun "wanders" back and forth between the Tropic of Cancer and Tropic of Capricorn. Air masses and wind systems shift in response.

*The satellite photo shows a spiral of clouds above the British Isles. The center of the low-pressure area is located above Ireland. An occlusion, which splits into a warm and a cold front, extends from that center. The warm front pushes a broad band of clouds ahead of itself; the cold front has only a relatively narrow cloud band. Reddish colors suggest warming in parts of the ocean.*

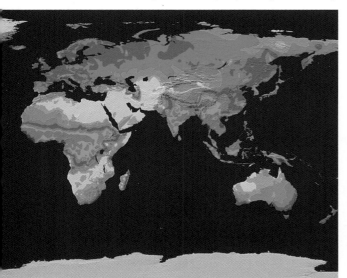

Average amounts of precipitation per month: September

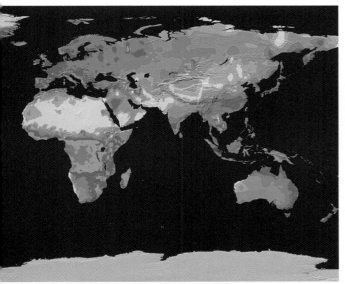

Average amounts of precipitation per month: November

Low-pressure area (cyclone) above the British Isles

# The Earth Endangered by Storms

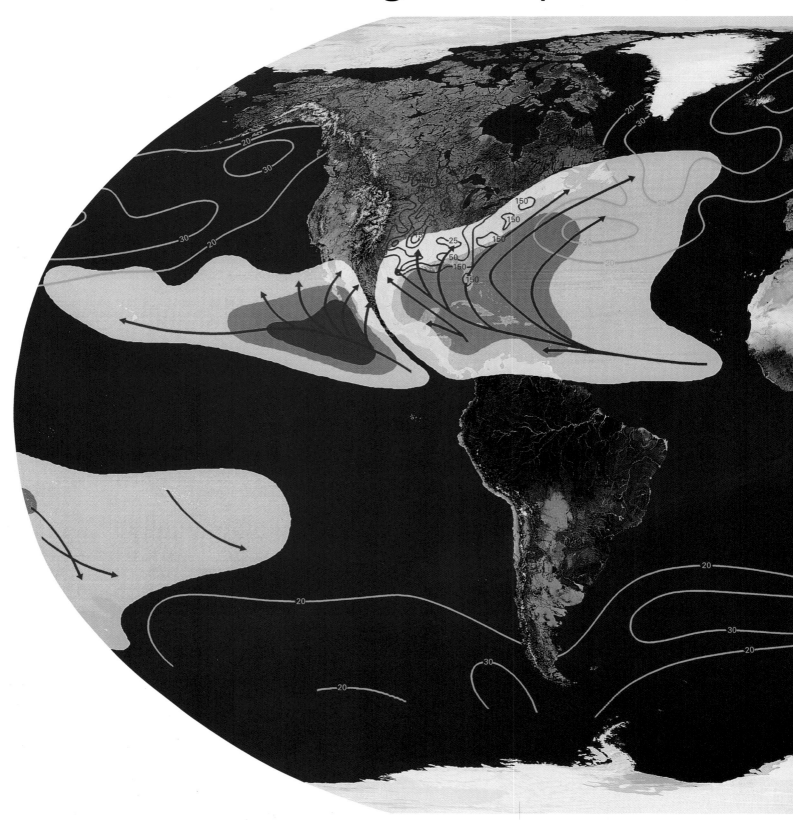

**Tropical Cyclones**

| | up to one per year | | more than 3 per year |
| | 1 to 3 per year | | average course |

**Tornadoes**

average interval of repetition per century

**Winter Storms**

frequency in percent

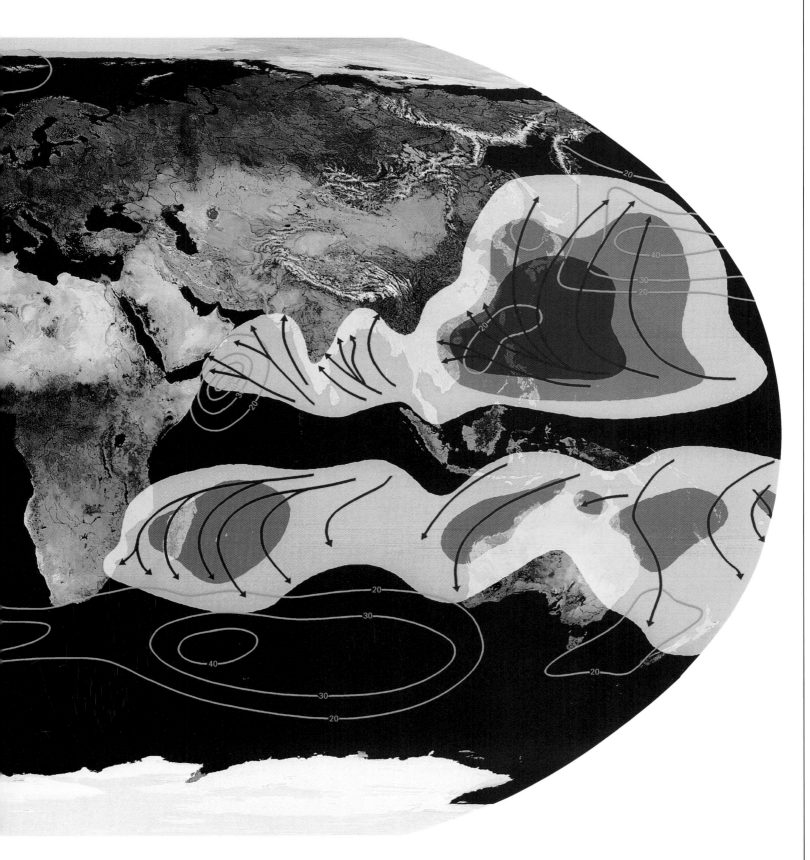

Tropical cyclones are born in summer and early autumn at latitudes between 5 and 10 degrees north and south of the Equator. They generally move westward at first, then curve northward (or southward) when they near a continent, before joining the westward drift. In this zone, west winds in winter frequently attain storm intensity, especially in the Southern Hemisphere, where they are not blocked by landmasses.

The rotating tunnels of North America's tornadoes are created when cold and warm air masses collide in the lee of the Rocky Mountains.

# Sandstorm over the Persian Gulf

The satellite photo shows part of the Arabian peninsula in late spring. Turkey, northern Iran, the Caspian Sea, and Turkmenistan form the northern border of the image. Mountainous Iran, Iraq (with its many reservoirs between the Tigris and Euphrates), and the Hedjas and Asir Mountains on the western edge of Arabia are all readily visible. To the south, one can see two straits: Bab el Mandeb between Arabia and Africa, and the Strait of Hormuz between Iran and Arabia. The center of the photo shows the stepped, layered landscape of central Saudi Arabia.

Note the distribution of white veils, which represent dust-laden air masses or clouds. Air masses are being drawn toward a weak, warm, springtime, low-pressure system above southeastern Iran and southern Pakistan. The dry air masses from the northwest cause long pennants of sand and dust, which appear like white veils above Arabia. Under the influence of the hot low-pressure system, warm moist air from the northern Indian Ocean changes from a southeast trade wind to a southwest monsoon, which creates clouds on the southern coast of Oman, but these clouds soon dissipate above the arid desert.

High temperatures and low humidity have desiccated much of the soil in Saudi Arabia. The country's sparse vegetation offers but little resistance to the strong winds. Periodically reappearing wadis seldom bring their freight of sediments all the way to the ocean; after the evaporation of the water, most of this sediment is left behind in inland basins that have no outlets. This process creates mighty regions of sand and fine sediments, constantly formed and reformed by the force of the wind.

The plume of sand visible in the photo is some 1,200 miles (2,000 kilometers) long. Dust particles in sandstorms often reach heights of more than 3,300 feet (1,000 meters). As the violet-colored stripes near the coastline reveal, these sandstorms can even cross narrow stretches of ocean without loss of intensity.

On land, the sandy areas in the Arabian Desert are sculpted by the wind into variously shaped dunes. In regions where winds blow from the same direction for many weeks each year, elongated lines of dunes are formed parallel to the direction of the predominant winds (stripe dunes). When some vegetation is present, the dunes develop perpendicular to the wind's direction and form the familiar fields of crescent dunes known as barchanes. If the wind direction varies, lines of dunes can grow together to create star-shaped dunes.

Even in sparsely settled Saudi Arabia, dust and sandstorms have always been a serious burden on the population. They endanger fisheries on the Gulf and may prevent boats from leaving port for days on end. Sandstorms bury waterholes, which are vital to the survival of wandering nomads, and they spread sand over the fertile land near oases. In recent years, they have seriously interfered with air and road traffic. Saudi Arabia has initiated large-scale projects to stabilize migratory dunes. Oases and areas near roads have been sprayed with crude oil, whose viscous texture helps to hold the sand in place. Windscreens of salt-resistant, fast-growing tamarisk have been planted to try to reduce wind speeds and thus stem the movement of the dunes.

If the earth's atmosphere were to become warmer, storm activity would increase and desertification would leave larger areas of land vulnerable and exposed to wind erosion.

*The reddish gray wall that looms behind this bus on a desert track in southern Iran announces the imminent arrival of a sandstorm. The storm will bury roads and hold people in "house arrest" inside their hermetically sealed homes. The high electric charge in the air, caused by the rubbing of one grain of sand against another, tends to make both animals and humans aggressive.*

Scale of the map segment: 1 to 80,000,000

| 0 | 800 | 1600 | 2400 | 3200 | 4000 km |

| 0 | 800 | 1600 | 2400 | 3000 Statute Miles |

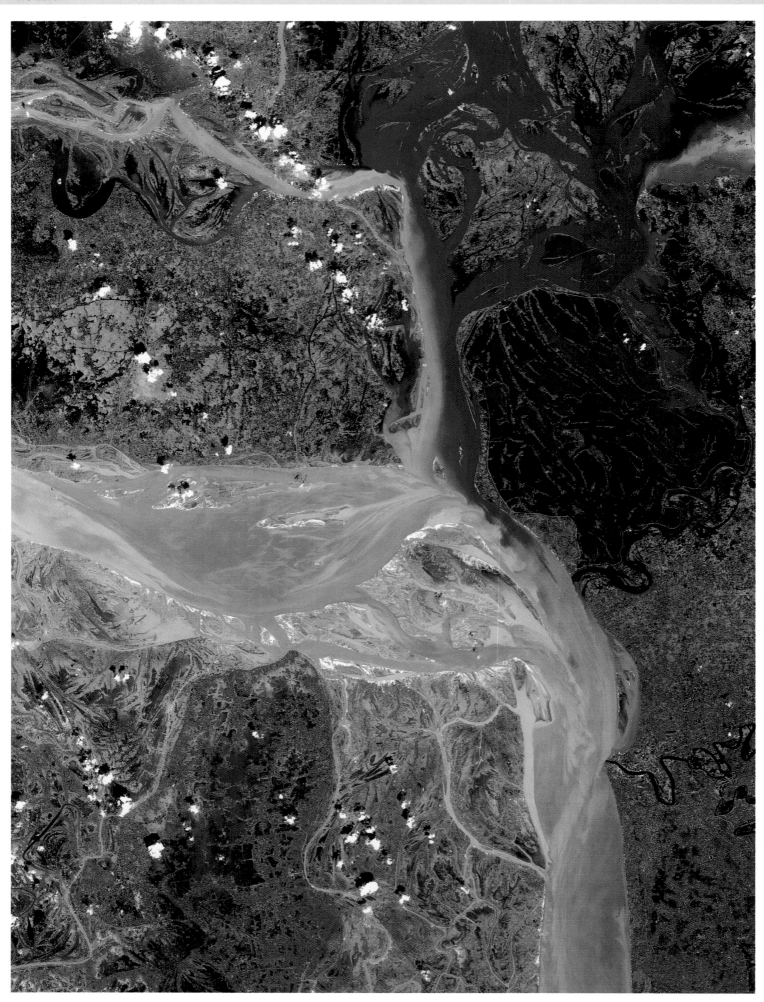

# Bangladesh: A Nation Prone to Flooding

Bangladesh is a moist, "amphibious" country. Its lowlands, which are almost entirely flat, are subject to periodic flooding. The satellite photo documents the situation during a "normal" high-water interval in East Bengal.

Flooding and subsequent deposition of sediments by the Ganges and Brahmaputra (Jamuna) Rivers have created a mighty river delta. The photo shows the water-rich arm of the Ganges (Padma) arriving from the west to join the Meghna. The Padma is some 6 miles (10 kilometers) wide here; the Meghna measures about 3 miles (5 kilometers) in width at the point where it leaves the photo toward the south.

Countless water arteries weave their way through the Ganges-Brahmaputra Delta. During the dry season, some of these dry up to become muddy meanders; oxbow lakes are replenished by seasonal floods. When waters are high, however, the mud-laden rivers cause widespread erosion, which leads them to constantly change their courses. Sandbanks are heaped up, mud islands are formed, bordering levees are carried away.

Between the depressions of the rivers and currents, older river terraces form broad "interfluvial plates," which are flooded only during intervals of extremely high water. People have built their villages on these slightly higher natural elevations or on artificially raised hills where they are protected from normal floodwaters. Nearly three-quarters of the east Bengali lowlands are regularly flooded.

Periodic flooding begins annually in midsummer and reaches its maximum in August, when the combination of heavy monsoon rains and water from melting Himalayan snows and glaciers raises the rivers. Flooding, however, does not usually occur unless storms and flood tides along

the coast prevent the monsoon rainwater and Himalayan meltwater from draining into the ocean. Under such conditions, the water level can rise as high as 21 feet (7 meters) to cover almost the entire lowlands. Catastrophic flooding of this sort occurred in 1970 and 1991; each disaster claimed some 300,000 lives, as well as leaving millions of people injured and homeless.

The people who inhabit this region have adapted their way of life and their means of earning a living to the conditions of a monsoon climate. Otherwise, it would be impossible for the moist country to support a population density that far exceeds 1,300 people per square mile (500 people per square kilometer). This density, one of the world's highest, is all the more remarkable when one considers that the population

*Farm families in the Ganges Delta live on artificially raised, earthen hills – like this one near Dhaka, the capital city. Low, narrow dikes surround the fields and pre-vent them from being destroyed by "normal" floods. During the dry season, these dikes maintain the level of water in the fields.*

here lives almost solely from farming. Low dikes (visible in the eastern-central portion of the photo) insure that the water level remains more or less constant during the rainy and dry seasons. This in turn makes it possible to harvest crops (especially rice) several times each year. Types of rice that are resistant to high water, as well as sorts that can grow when water levels are low, have both been planted here. Rice is the major subsistence crop; jute is the most important marketed crop.

Narayanganj, at the northern edge of the photo, is the only larger settlement visible. It is located about 19 miles south (30 kilometers) of Dhaka at the confluence of the Lakhia and Dhaleswari Rivers. With more than 100,000 inhabitants, the city's importance as a center for the manufacture of jute products, as chief seat of the jute authorities, as a site of jute mills and looms, and as a significant river harbor are all due to its favorable location in Bengal's network of rivers. River transport is the most convenient means of transportation in this low-lying country.

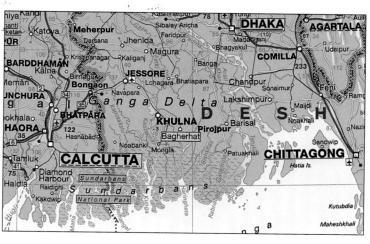

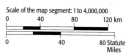

Scale of the map segment: 1 to 4,000,000

0    40    80    120 km

0              40          80 Statute Miles

57

# The Distribution of Temperatures

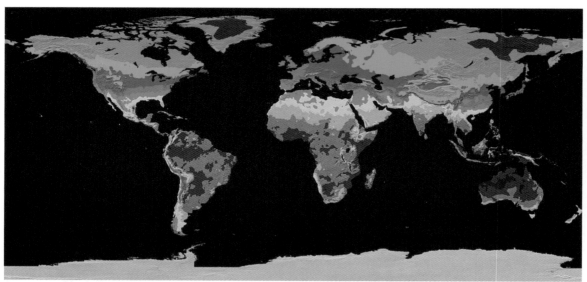
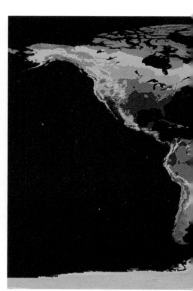

Average Monthly Air Temperature: January

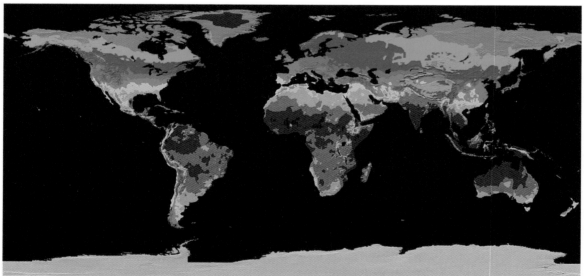
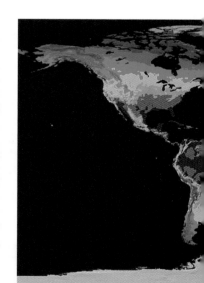

Average Monthly Air Temperature: March

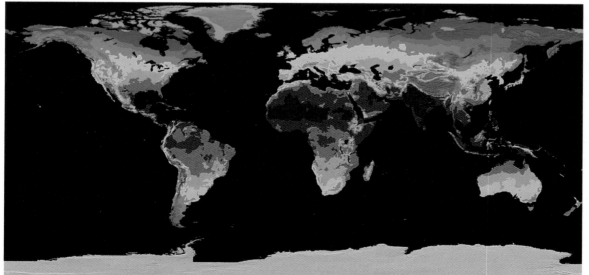

Average Monthly Air Temperature: May

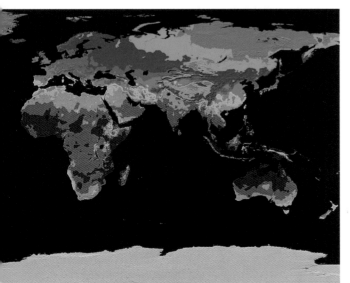

Average Monthly Air Temperature: July

Average Monthly Air Temperature: September

Average Monthly Air Temperature: November

## Average Monthly Air Temperature Below Freezing

### Below freezing

| | |
|---|---|
| ■ | 76 – 58 °Fahrenheit |
| ■ | 58 – 40 °Fahrenheit |
| ■ | 40 – 4 °Fahrenheit |
| ■ | 4 – 14 °Fahrenheit |
| ■ | 14 – 32 °Fahrenheit |

### Above freezing

| | |
|---|---|
| | 32 – 41 °Fahrenheit |
| ■ | 41 – 50 °Fahrenheit |
| ■ | 50 – 59 °Fahrenheit |
| ■ | 59 – 68 °Fahrenheit |
| ■ | 68 – 77 °Fahrenheit |
| ■ | 77 – 86 °Fahrenheit |
| ■ | 86 – 95 °Fahrenheit |
| ■ | 95 – 104 °Fahrenheit and warmer |

Measurements taken during a 30-month period at 6,280 weather stations around the world were used to create this graphic depiction of average monthly temperatures on land. Especially evident here is the interaction between two phenomena: first, the shifts of bands of temperature that run parallel to the lines of latitude as a consequence of the sun's apparent north-south wandering during the course of the years; second, the influences on local temperature conditions caused by distinctive patterns of land-ocean distribution, ocean currents, cloud cover, and topographical relief. The situation of Eurasia can serve as an example. The southward intrusion of cold, polar air masses during the northern winter is hindered here by the warm Gulf Stream, whose influence extends far into eastern Europe. The cold Oya Schio, which influences the climate of eastern Asia, supports the advance of polar air. Western and northern Europe experience generally warmer temperatures than do places located at comparable latitudes in Asia and North America. High mountains appear as cold-weather islands throughout the year. The cooling effect of ocean currents, for example, the Benguela and Humboldt (Peru) Currents, is visible along the southwestern coasts of Africa and South America.

*Estimates of temperature trends in the world's temperate climatic zones suggest that the Earth has become warmer during the last 15,000 years. Some scientists believe that the temperature curve has reached a plateau that will be followed by a new Ice Age, similar to the one that ended about 10,000 years ago.*

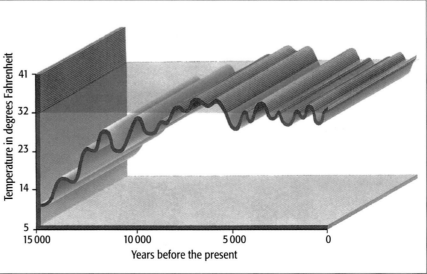

Temperature Trend

# Southern Föhn in the Alps

This satellite photo depicts an area in Austria stretching from the Inn River in the Alpine foothills, across the northern Kalk Alps and the longitudinal valley of Pinzgau and the Upper Enns Valley, to the Hohe Tauern.

The northern part of the Alpine foothills is cloudless. The upper reaches of the high mountain ranges are covered with snow. The Niedere Tauern is hidden beneath clouds (southeastern corner of the photo) as are the northernmost mountain ranges. Several "lakes" of cold air fill the Upper Enns Valley.

This distribution of clouds is a result of the föhn, a mountain wind associated with short-term variations in barometric pressure. The föhn causes temperatures to rise,

*A föhn wall "stands" atop a high ridge of the Alps in the Schladminger Tauern. From here, the air will glide downward into the valley. As it descends, it grows warmer, and this warm- ing causes increased evaporation and dissipa- tion of clouds. The flat upper boundary of the cloud layer indicates the stable stratification of the air windward of the mountains.*

clouds to dissipate, evaporation to increase, and relative humidity to decrease. Intensive solar radiation and clear visibility are further effects of the föhn.

The föhn is caused by the barrier effect of a mountain range perpendicular to the direction an air mass is moving. When high pressure conditions with stable layers of air occur south of the Alps, and a southwesterly current establishes itself north of the Alps, a perpendicular current begins above the mountain ridges. A "föhn wall" with "stalled clouds" forms. In the lee of the mountain ranges, air descends from 6,500 to 10,000 feet (2,000 to 3,000 meter) elevations into Alpine valleys and foothills, growing warmer in a dry, adiabatic process.

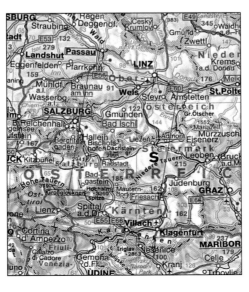

*This false-color temper- ature image uses a psy- chological spectrum of colors: high tempera- tures are shown as red, lower temperatures as blue to white shades.*

*The föhn has already reached and warmed in- dividual low-lying val- leys, but has not yet dis- placed the heavier "lakes" of cold air in the upper portions of the valleys.*

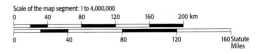

Scale of the map segment: 1 to 4,000,000

# Model Simulating Global Effects o

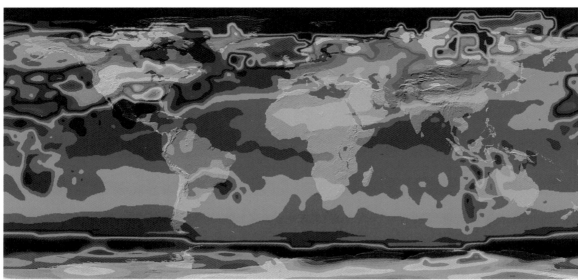

Simulation: temperature change with doubled amount of $CO_2$ in the atmosphere: summer

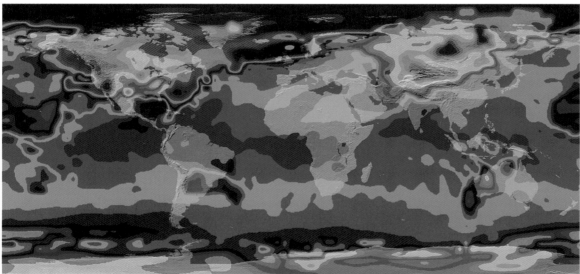

Simulation: temperature change with doubled amount of $CO_2$ in the atmosphere: winter

**Simulation: temperature change with doubled amount of $CO_2$ in the atmosphere**

Temperature reduction

| ■ | 3.6 – 0.0 °Fahrenheit |

Temperature increase

| ■ | 0.0 – 0.9 °Fahrenheit |
| ■ | 0.9 – 1.8 °Fahrenheit |
| ■ | 1.8 – 2.7 °Fahrenheit |
| ■ | 2.7 – 3.6 °Fahrenheit |
| ■ | 3.6 – 4.5 °Fahrenheit |
| ■ | 4.5 – 5.4 °Fahrenheit |
| ■ | 5.4 – 6.3 °Fahrenheit |
| ■ | 6.3 – 7.2 °Fahrenheit |
| ■ | 7.2 – 8.1 °Fahrenheit |
| ■ | 8.1 – 9.0 °Fahrenheit |
| ■ | 9.0 – 9.9 °Fahrenheit |
| ■ | 9.9 – 10.8 °Fahrenheit |
| ■ | 10.8 – 12.6 °Fahrenheit |
| ■ | 12.6 – 14.4 °Fahrenheit |
| ■ | 14.4 – 16.2 °Fahrenheit |
| ■ | 16.2 – 18.0 °Fahrenheit |
| ■ | 18.0 – 19.8 °Fahrenheit |
| ■ | 19.8 – 21.6 °Fahrenheit |
| ■ | 21.6 – 25.2 °Fahrenheit |
| ■ | 25.2 – 28.8 °Fahrenheit |
| ■ | 28.8 – 32.4 °Fahrenheit |
| ■ | 32.4 – 36.0 °Fahrenheit |
| □ | over 36.0 °Fahrenheit |

**Simulation: coastal regions endangered by rise in sea level due to doubled of $CO_2$ in the atmosphere**

| ■ | Endangered coastal regions |

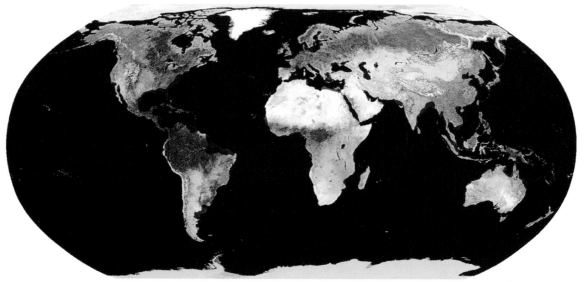

Simulation: coastal regions endangered by rise in sea level due to doubled of $CO_2$ in the atmosphere

# Doubled Concentration of CO₂

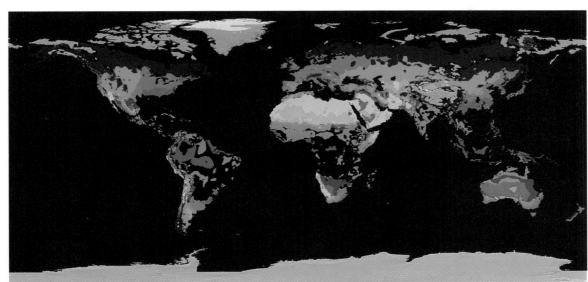

Present-day vegetation zones (according to Holdridge)

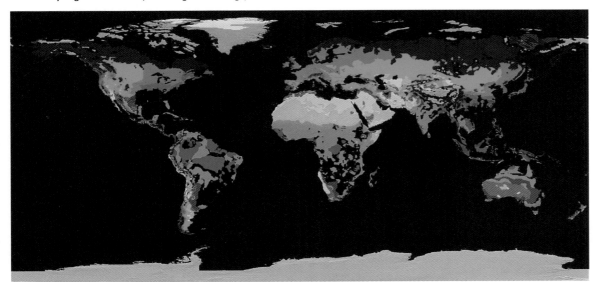

Simulation: vegetation zones (according to Holdridge) with doubled amount of CO₂ in the atmosphere

## Vegetation zones according to Holdridge

- Icy desert
- Cold desert
- Tundra
- Boreal coniferous forest
- Deciduous forests and steppes, of the temperature latitudes
- Winter-cold desert
- Winter-cold semidesert
- Summer-green deciduous forests
- Subtropical grasslands
- Subtropical forests
- Semideserts and deserts
- Grasslands of the intermittently wet tropics
- Forests of the permanently wet tropics

Carbon dioxide comprises 0.03 percent by volume and 0.04 percent by weight of the Earth's atmosphere. Carbon dioxide ($CO_2$) is formed as a product of plant (photosynthesis) and animal respiration, through alcoholic fermentation, and during the normal combustion of carbon-containing fuels. During photosynthesis, green plants use the energy of solar radiation to synthesize carbohydrates from $CO_2$ and water. Oxygen, which animals and humans alike must breathe, is set free during this process. But burning of fossil fuels and destruction of forests interfere with this natural cycle. Increased amounts of carbon dioxide in the air absorb more of the infrared radiation, which the Earth's surface partly absorbs and

largely reflects; air temperatures rise as a result. The amount of $CO_2$ in the air has increased from 280 ppm (parts per million) in 1750 to 335 ppm today. Between 1851 and 1987, the temperature of air near the ground has increased worldwide by 0.9 degrees Fahrenheit (0.5 degrees Celsius). This warming has caused sea level to rise between 3.9 and 5.9 inches (10 to 15 centimeters), increased the strength of low-pressure areas over the North Atlantic and North Pacific, and increased average wind speeds. Because of the growing energy requirements (especially in the industrialized nations), continued increases in the level of $CO_2$ emissions are to be expected.

# The Shrinking of the Inland Glaciers: The Grossglockner

The Glockner Group is located in the Hohe Tauern mountain range, which includes, Austria's highest peak, the Grossglockner (12,457 feet = 3,797 meters) and its longest glacier, the Pasterze (6 miles = 9 kilometers). Stubach, Kapruner, and Fuscher Valleys extend from the Glockner Group to the north; Dorfer and Möll Valleys extend southward. These valleys all received their present appearance as trough valleys with glacial pans (Tauern moss, waterfall ground, Mooser ground) from the Ice-Age glaciers.

During cold periods, a solid network of slowly flowing ice covered the Alps. The surface of that sheet reached heights of some 7,200 feet (2,200 meters) during the Ice Age. During the subsequent warm period, the glaciers retreated to their present size and position. When the climate cooled between the 16th and mid-19th centuries, the glaciers advanced again. At that time, the snout of the Karlinger Kees glacier was nearly a mile (1.5 kilometers) longer than it is today, reaching to the present shore of Mooserboden Reservoir. Masses of debris on both sides of the Pasterzenkes, wall-shaped moraines, and pioneer vegetation just below the snout are proof that the glacier has been melting and retreating for about 150 years, although the retreat was interrupted by minor advances around 1880, 1920, and from the mid-1950s to the 1970s. Cool summers and abundant snowfall led to an increase in the mass of snow and ice in the glacier's tributary region. This increase only becomes apparent at the

lower end of the glacier after a lag of several years. Glaciers change in response to changes in mass, which in turn are closely related to climatic changes.

To open the region to tourism, the Grossglockner high alpine road was opened in 1935. Further access to the high-mountain region was provided by the installation of the reservoir stairs in Kapruner and Stubach Valleys. The causes for the establishment of annual reservoirs were the great potential energy in the land's topography, the high precipitation on the north slope of the mountain range, and the heavy glaciation.

*Longitudinal and transverse crevices form the shield of the Pasterze. With an area of about 6.9 square miles (18 square kilometers) and a length of more than 5 miles (8 kilometers), this is the largest glacier in the eastern Alps. The Pasterze has lost more than one-third of its area since 1850, and it continues to retreat today. Annual measurements quantify the course of changes in the glacier, not solely because of scientific interest, but also because the glacier is an important source of energy.*

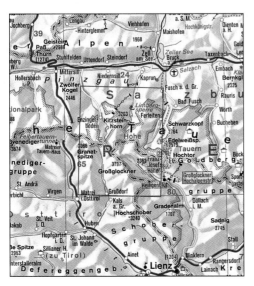

Scale of the map segment: 1 to 800,000

0    8    16    24    32    40 km

0    8    16    24    30 Statute Miles

# Wind Speeds over the Oceans

Northern Summer

Winds are currents of air that balance out local and planetary difference in pressure. They reach their highest speeds over the oceans where they are free from the influences of friction with the ground and are neither blocked by nor forced to detour around mountain chains. Because they moderate and cool temperatures and because of their importance as a means of refreshing air, winds are a significant climatic factor.

Comparison between the two depictions shows seasonal shifts in wind systems and changes in their speed. Calm zones where there is almost no wind are largest during each hemisphere's summer. In the winter, polar easterlies cause higher wind speeds in the extratropical west wind circulation.

## Wind Speeds

- 0 – 3.3 feet per second
- 3.3 – 6.6 feet per second
- 6.6 – 9.8 feet per second
- 9.8 – 13.1 feet per second
- 13.1 – 16.4 feet per second
- 16.4 – 19.7 feet per second
- 19.7 – 23.0 feet per second
- 23.0 – 26.2 feet per second
- 26.2 – 29.5 feet per second
- 29.5 – 32.8 feet per second
- 32.8 – 36.0 feet per second
- 36.0 – 39.4 feet per second
- 39.4 – 42.6 feet per second
- 42.6 – 45.9 feet per second and faster

Northern Winter

| Beaufort Scale | Description | Maritime effects | Miles per hour (mph) | Knots (kn) |
|---|---|---|---|---|
| 0 | Calm | Mirror-flat sea | 0.0 – 0.5 | 0 – 1 |
| 1 | Gentle zephyr | Small, scale-shaped waves without whitecaps | 0.5 – 3.4 | 1 – 2 |
| 2 | Light breeze | Small waves, short but more clearly visible; wave peaks still look glassy and do not yet break | 3.4 – 7.4 | 3 – 5 |
| 3 | Weak breeze | Wave peaks begin to break; foam mostly glassy; occasional small whitecaps may appear | 7.4 – 12.1 | 6 – 9 |
| 4 | Moderate breeze | Waves still small, but getting longer; whitecaps appearing with greater frequency | 12.1 – 17.6 | 10 – 13 |
| 5 | Fresh breeze | Moderate waves which assume a clearly elongated shape; whitecaps everywhere; some foam | 17.6 – 23.9 | 14 – 18 |
| 6 | Strong wind | Large waves begin to form; wave peaks break and leave larger, more extensive areas of white suds; some foam | 23.9 – 30.9 | 19 – 24 |
| 7 | Stiff wind | Sea rises into towering waves; when waves break, the resulting foam begins to stretch itself in strips in the direction of the wind | 30.9 – 38.3 | 25 – 30 |
| 8 | Stormy wind | Medium-high wave hills with long ridges, some foam blowing off the ridges | 38.3 – 46.3 | 31 – 37 |
| 9 | Storm | High wave hills; dense strips of foam in direction of wind; sea begins to "roll"; foam can limit visibility | 46.3 – 54.6 | 38 – 44 |
| 10 | Heavy storm | Very high wave hills; ridges breaking over; white foam "rolls" abruptly; poor visibility | 54.6 – 63.5 | 45 – 52 |
| 11 | Storm of hurricane intensity | Unusually high wave hills; visibility reduced by foam | 63.5 – 73.0 | 53 – 60 |
| 12 | Hurricane | Air filled with foam; sea entirely white; visibility severely reduced; no distant views possible | 73.0 – 82,5 | 61 – 88 |

*Wind speeds are still measured on a scale of 1 through 12 based on visible changes in the environment. This familiar descriptive system is now seldom used by meteorologists because wind speeds in excess of Beaufort 12 have since been measured.*

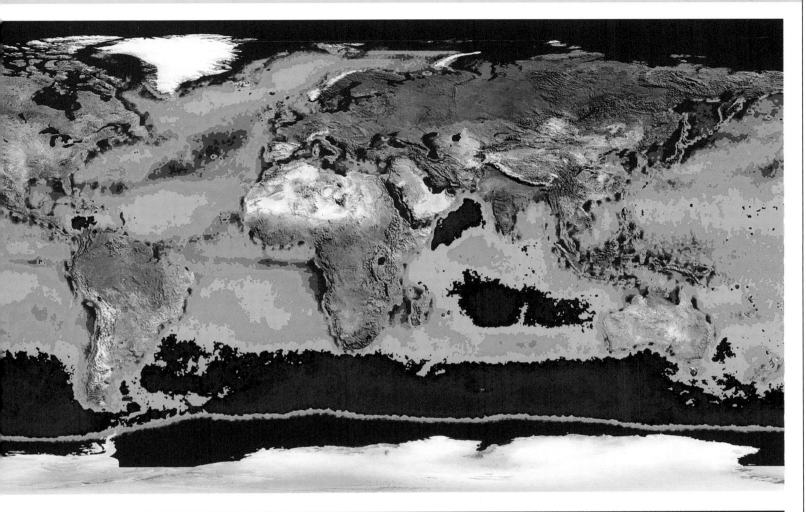

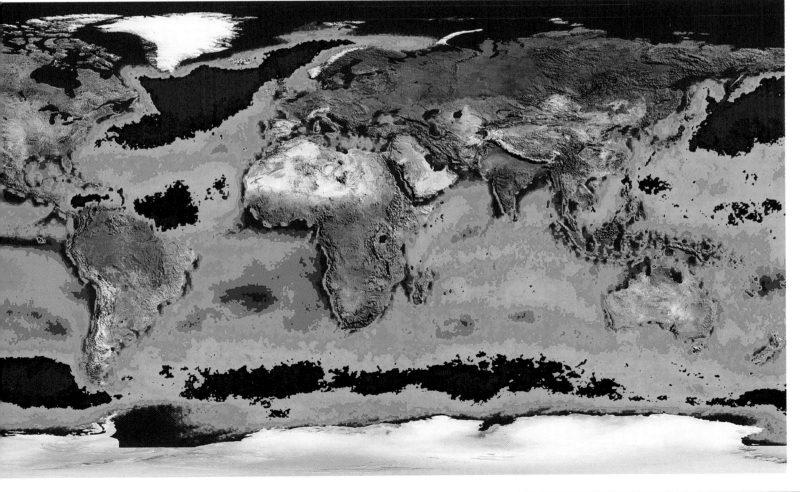

# Heights of Ocean Waves

From an altitude of approximately 620 miles (1,000 kilometers), the Geosat satellite measures the effects of atmospheric turbulence on the oceans within several inches. Changes in air pressure and winds are the primary causes of waves on the open ocean. Maps showing the height of ocean waves during particular seasons of the year reveal the following distribution of the Earth's wind belts: calm, almost windless zones near the Equator; ceaselessly blowing trade winds at higher latitudes; and nearly windless zones in the subtropical horse latitudes. The zones of greatest wave amplitude are especially striking. These include the west wind zone called the "Roaring Forties," which, during the northern summer, develops in the Southern Hemisphere where westerly winds often blow with hurricane intensity because there are hardly any obstacles (like continents) to reduce their speed. A parallel phenomenon occurs at the same latitudes in the Northern Hemisphere during northern winters.

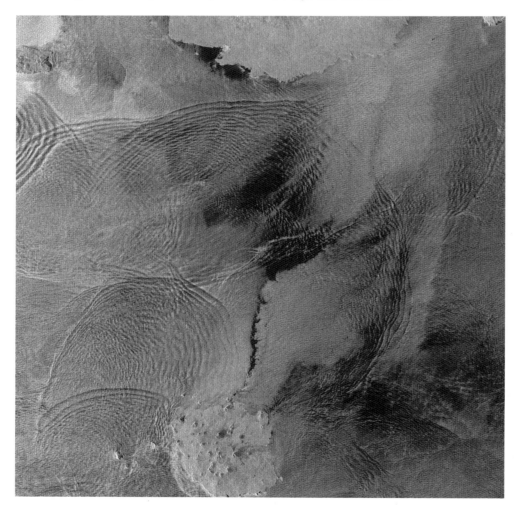

*Several similar groups of wave systems overlap one another near the Galapagos Islands in the Pacific Ocean not far from the Equator, between Floreana in the south and Santa Cruz in the north. Depending on the lengths of their phases, interference between waves can either increase wave intensity or cancel them out entirely.*

## Wave Heights

| | |
|---|---|
| ■ 0.3 – 1.6 feet | ▧ 9.8 – 11.5 feet |
| ■ 1.6 – 3.3 feet | ▧ 11.5 – 13.1 feet |
| ■ 3.3 – 4.9 feet | ■ 13.1 – 14.8 feet |
| ▨ 4.9 – 6.6 feet | ■ 14.8 – 16.4 feet |
| ▧ 6.6 – 8.2 feet | ■ 16.4 – 18.0 feet |
| ▧ 8.2 – 9.8 feet | ■ over 18.0 feet |
| | ■ no available data |

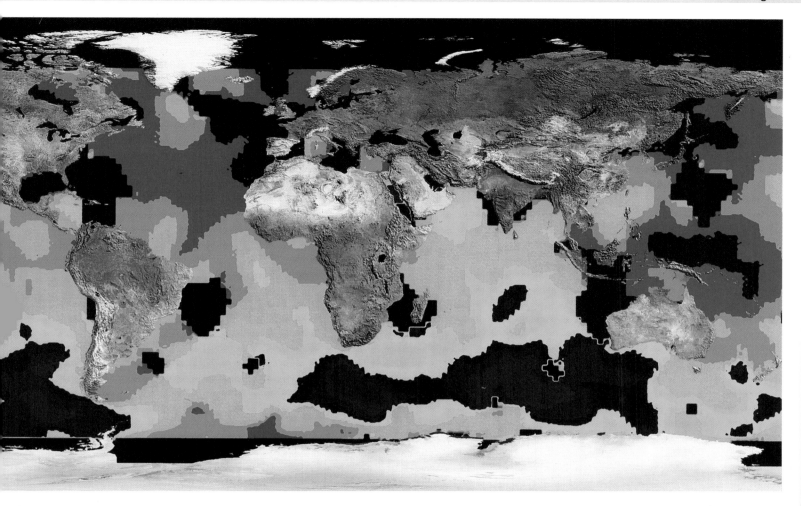

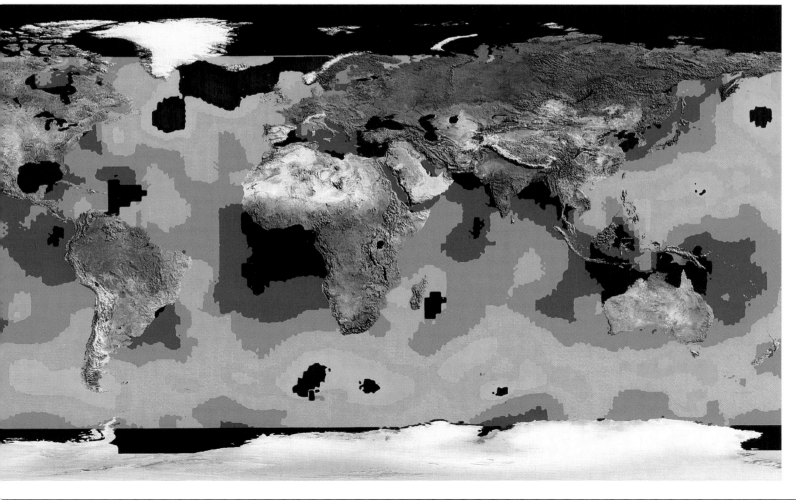

# Distribution of Ocean Surface Tempe

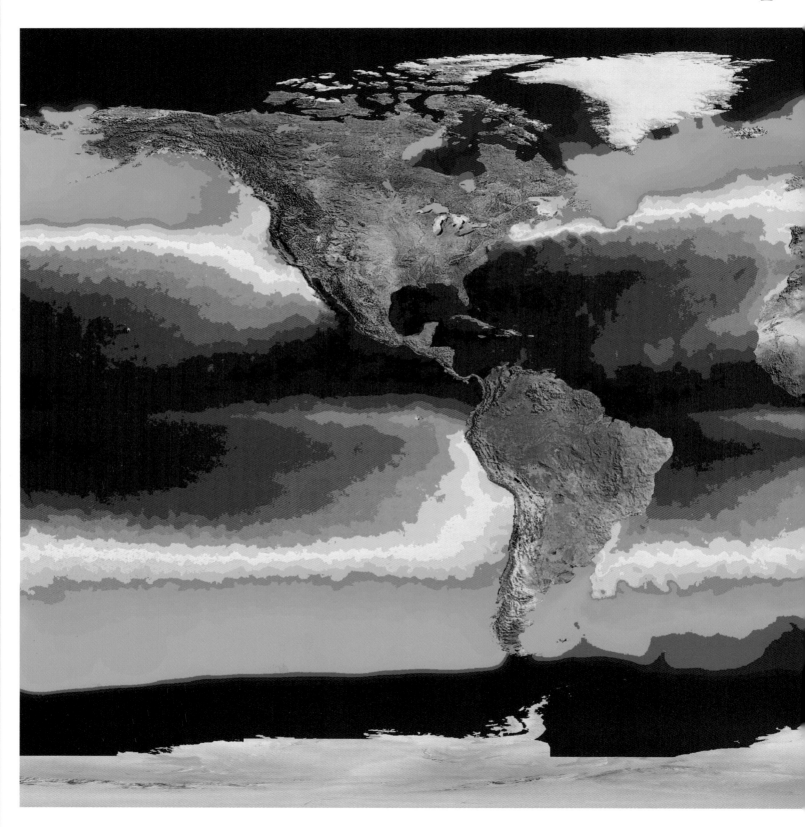

**Temperature of the Ocean
Surface (Summer)**

| | |
|---|---|
| ■ | 32.0 °Fahrenheit |
| ■ | 32.0 – 34.7 °Fahrenheit |
| ■ | 34.7 – 37.4 °Fahrenheit |
| ■ | 37.4 – 40.1 °Fahrenheit |
| ■ | 40.1 – 42.8 °Fahrenheit |
| ■ | 42.8 – 45.5 °Fahrenheit |
| ■ | 45.5 – 48.2 °Fahrenheit |
| ■ | 48.2 – 50.9 °Fahrenheit |
| ■ | 50.9 – 53.6 °Fahrenheit |
| ■ | 53.6 – 56.3 °Fahrenheit |
| ■ | 56.3 – 59.0 °Fahrenheit |
| ■ | 59.0 – 61.7 °Fahrenheit |
| ■ | 61.7 – 64.4 °Fahrenheit |
| ■ | 64.4 – 67.1 °Fahrenheit |

# tures in Summer

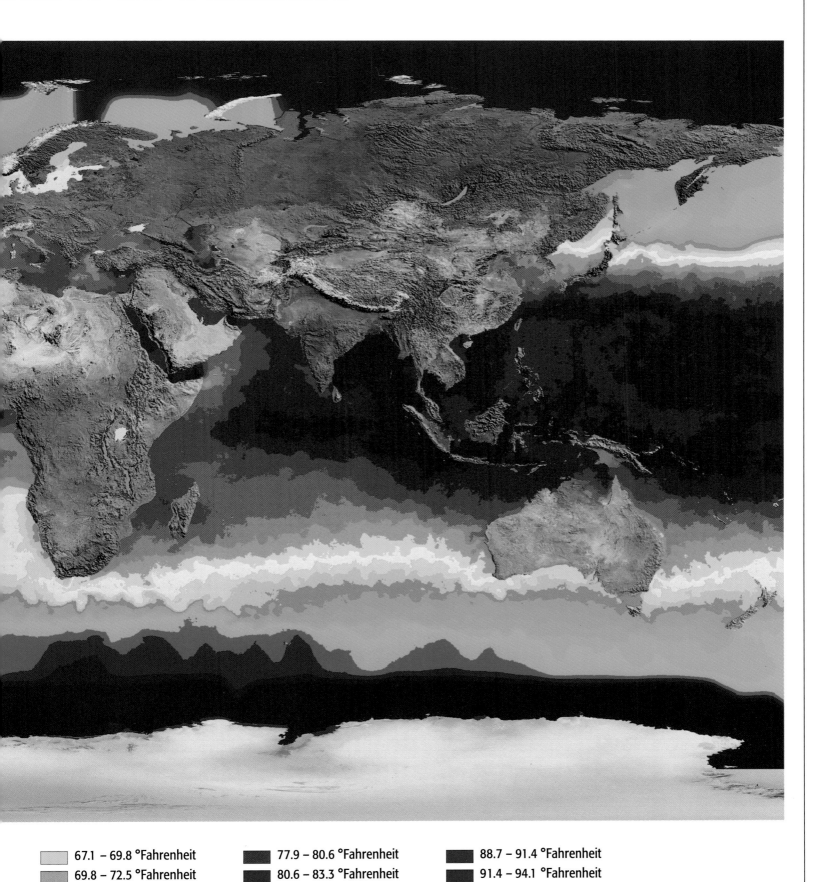

| | | |
|---|---|---|
| 67.1 – 69.8 °Fahrenheit | 77.9 – 80.6 °Fahrenheit | 88.7 – 91.4 °Fahrenheit |
| 69.8 – 72.5 °Fahrenheit | 80.6 – 83.3 °Fahrenheit | 91.4 – 94.1 °Fahrenheit |
| 72.5 – 76.8 °Fahrenheit | 83.3 – 86.0 °Fahrenheit | 94.1 – 96.8 °Fahrenheit |
| 76.8 – 77.9 °Fahrenheit | 86.0 – 88.7 °Fahrenheit | |

# Distribution of Ocean Surface Tempe

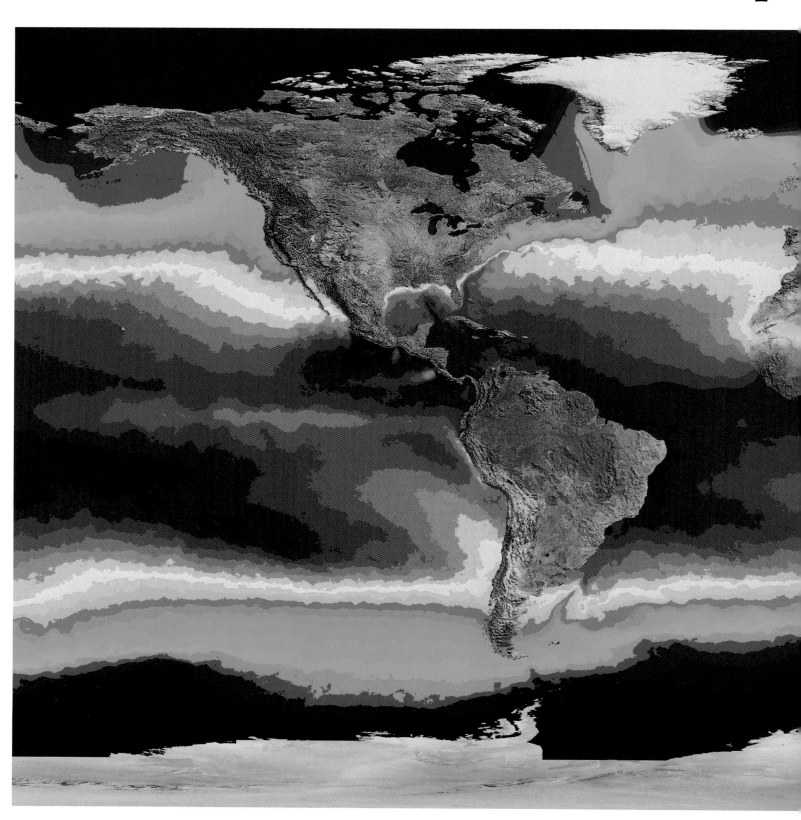

**Temperature of the**
**Ocean Surface (Winter)**

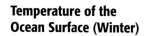

| | | |
|---|---|---|
| 32.0 °Fahrenheit | 34.7 – 37.4 °Fahrenheit | 45.5 – 48.2 °Fahrenheit | 56.3 – 59.0 °Fahrenheit |
| 32.0 – 34.7 °Fahrenheit | 37.4 – 40.1 °Fahrenheit | 48.2 – 50.9 °Fahrenheit | 59.0 – 61.7 °Fahrenheit |
| | 40.1 – 42.8 °Fahrenheit | 50.9 – 53.6 °Fahrenheit | 61.7 – 64.4 °Fahrenheit |
| | 42.8 – 45.5 °Fahrenheit | 53.6 – 56.3 °Fahrenheit | 64.4 – 67.1 °Fahrenheit |

# tures in Winter

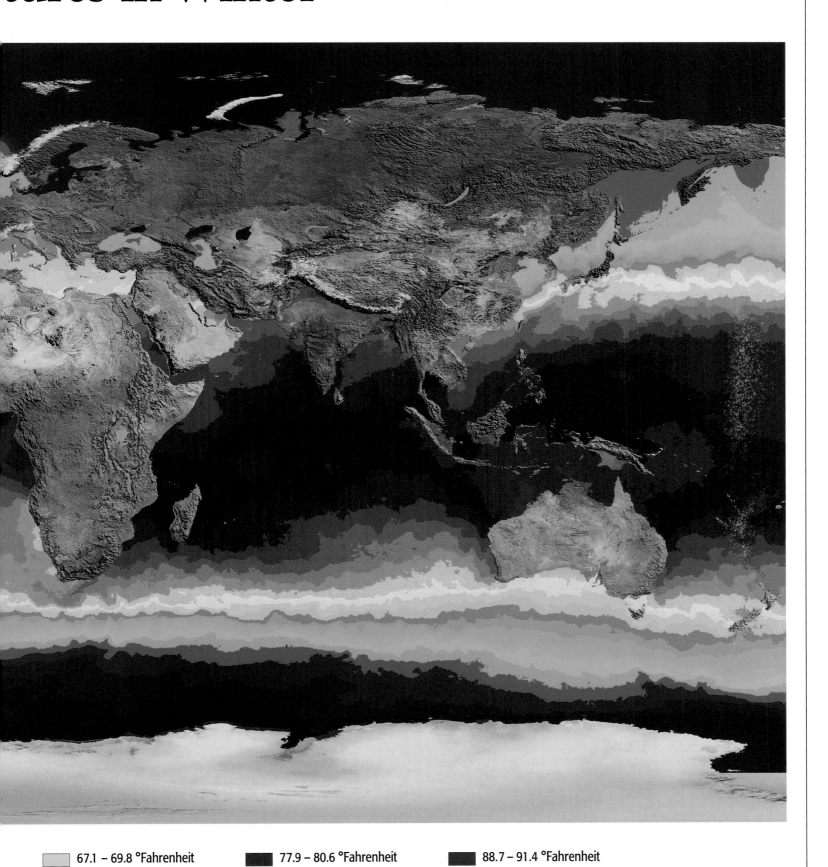

| | | | | | |
|---|---|---|---|---|---|
| 67.1 – 69.8 °Fahrenheit | | 77.9 – 80.6 °Fahrenheit | | 88.7 – 91.4 °Fahrenheit | |
| 69.8 – 72.5 °Fahrenheit | | 80.6 – 83.3 °Fahrenheit | | 91.4 – 94.1 °Fahrenheit | |
| 72.5 – 76.8 °Fahrenheit | | 83.3 – 86.0 °Fahrenheit | | 94.1 – 96.8 °Fahrenheit | |
| 76.8 – 77.9 °Fahrenheit | | 86.0 – 88.7 °Fahrenheit | | | |

# The El Niño Phenomenon

The "Christ Child" comes every year. El Niño, the little boy or the Christ Child, is the name of a warm coastal current that appears each year around Christmastime along the Pacific Coast of Peru. But at intervals of from 4 to 30 years, this "Christ Child" develops diabolical energies and brings torrential rains to an ordinarily arid coastal plain.

The principal causes for the El Niño phenomenon are a pair of air-pressure systems – the Australian-Asian low and the South Pacific high-pressure system – which always behave as opposites. When atmospheric pressure in the South Pacific is particularly high, barometers in the Australian-Asian region yield particularly low readings, and vice versa. This distribution of air pressure, together with a pair of circulation cells, is responsible for the El Niño effect.

One of these cells is influenced by warm air rising in the equatorial belt. This air

flows toward the poles, begins to descend around 30° North and South latitudes, then returns toward the Equator as the familiar trade winds. The second circulation cell is composed of air masses that flow from east to west at low altitudes near the Equator, then return eastward at higher elevations. The low-altitude portion of this cell pushes warm surface water ahead of itself toward the west with enough force to raise sea level in the Asian-Australian region by as much as 9.8 inches (25 centimeters). This westward displacement is compensated by the Humboldt Current, cold, highly oxygenated, nutrient-rich water that rises off the South American coast. Changes in the gradient of atmospheric pressure between an Asian-Australian low and a South Pacific high can significantly weaken the entire system of air-mass exchange: warm water "slips back" eastward, where it warms air masses. The rising arm of the large-scale

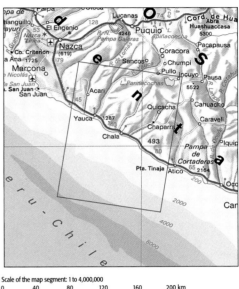

Scale of the map segment: 1 to 4,000,000

air-circulation cell shifts toward the western coast of South America, where it causes intense precipitation; Australia and Asia, on the other hand, suffer severe droughts.

Images depicting temperatures in the Pacific Ocean in 1987 clearly show the El Niño phenomenon. Warm water (yellow and red tones) penetrates a long way toward the South American coast.

The satellite image shows cloud formation off the Peruvian coast characteristic of an El Niño year: warm rising air masses with abundant condensation.

Temperature distribution on September 9, 1986

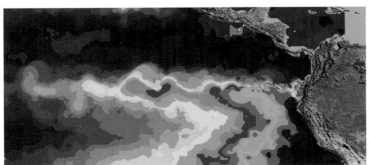

Temperature distribution on September 5, 1987

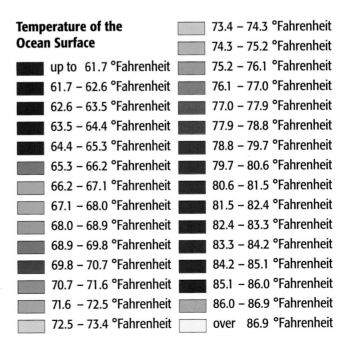

Temperature distribution on September 6, 1988

**Temperature of the Ocean Surface**

| | |
|---|---|
| up to 61.7 °Fahrenheit | 73.4 – 74.3 °Fahrenheit |
| 61.7 – 62.6 °Fahrenheit | 74.3 – 75.2 °Fahrenheit |
| 62.6 – 63.5 °Fahrenheit | 75.2 – 76.1 °Fahrenheit |
| 63.5 – 64.4 °Fahrenheit | 76.1 – 77.0 °Fahrenheit |
| 64.4 – 65.3 °Fahrenheit | 77.0 – 77.9 °Fahrenheit |
| 65.3 – 66.2 °Fahrenheit | 77.9 – 78.8 °Fahrenheit |
| 66.2 – 67.1 °Fahrenheit | 78.8 – 79.7 °Fahrenheit |
| 67.1 – 68.0 °Fahrenheit | 79.7 – 80.6 °Fahrenheit |
| 68.0 – 68.9 °Fahrenheit | 80.6 – 81.5 °Fahrenheit |
| 68.9 – 69.8 °Fahrenheit | 81.5 – 82.4 °Fahrenheit |
| 69.8 – 70.7 °Fahrenheit | 82.4 – 83.3 °Fahrenheit |
| 70.7 – 71.6 °Fahrenheit | 83.3 – 84.2 °Fahrenheit |
| 71.6 – 72.5 °Fahrenheit | 84.2 – 85.1 °Fahrenheit |
| 72.5 – 73.4 °Fahrenheit | 85.1 – 86.0 °Fahrenheit |
| | 86.0 – 86.9 °Fahrenheit |
| | over 86.9 °Fahrenheit |

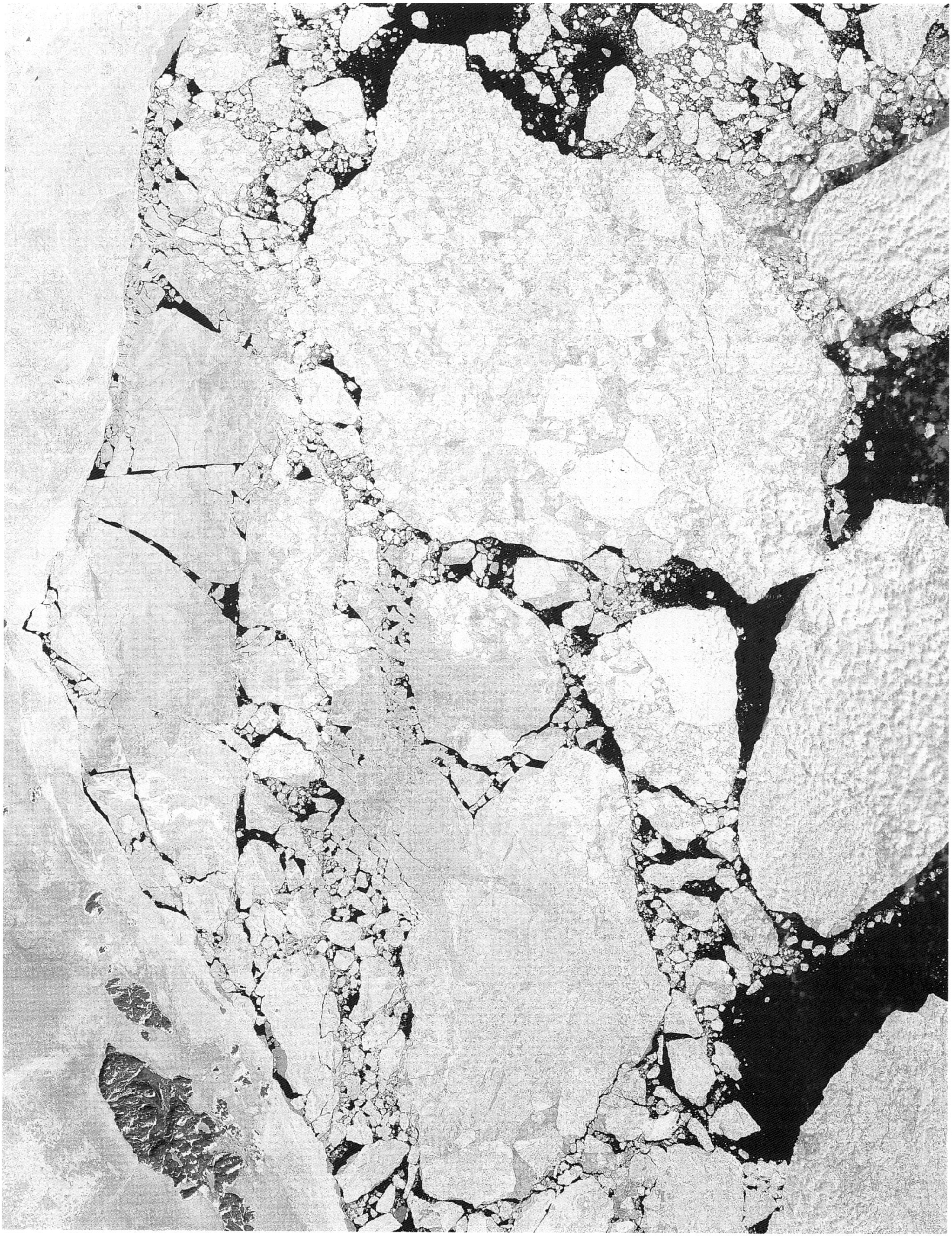

# Ice in the Arctic Ocean

The satellite photo shows a segment of the eastern coast of Greenland during the summer. Along the picture's western edge lies a belt of shelf ice that is firmly attached to Greenland and to some small islands (lower left). Pack ice – large plates of floating ice – is found farther offshore. Pale blue areas in the photo represent newly formed ice.

For many years, only adventurers, imperialist or expansionist politicians, and natural-resource prospectors were especially interested in the polar regions. Only recently have the polar ice masses been discovered as an archive of the Earth's climatic history. The ice preserves a record of the atmosphere's gaseous composition, dust,

sity of its waters so significantly that no water would sink to great depths and no longer create the suction that has thus-far drawn warm, tropical water toward western and northern Europe in the Gulf Stream. Reduction of a mere 0.6 percent in the volume of salt would suffice to stop the large-scale circulation.

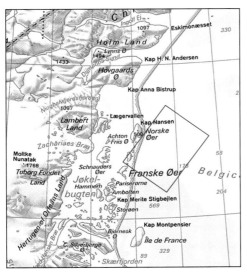

and even pollen for thousands of years. It also comprises a huge reserve of freshwater, which, when it freezes or melts, can cause or exert a tremendous influence on ocean currents, air-mass movements, and changes in the height of sea level. Melting and freezing in the polar zones also offer important clues about long-term global temperature tendencies.

According to one geoclimatic scenario, ice melting in the northern polar region would add so much freshwater to the Arctic Ocean, thus reducing its concentration of salt so drastically and changing the den-

*The photo shows drifting ice in Jakobshaven ice fjord off the eastern coast of Greenland. The color of the ice in the middle of the picture indicates that these are icebergs spawned by calving glaciers. Most*

*icebergs in the Arctic Ocean are small and irregularly shaped. Icebergs born in Antarctica are often made of shelf ice and are correspondingly larger, with flattened upper surfaces.*

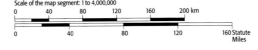

Scale of the map segment: 1 to 4,000,000

0    40    80    120    160    200 km

0         40         80         120        160 Statute Miles

# Distribution of Phyto-plankton in the Oceans

Summer

The concentration of phytoplankton in seawater is subject to seasonal variations because the production of this form of plant life depends on the amount of sunlight penetrating the seawater, as well as on the salinity and temperature of the water. Phytoplankton's habitat is the well-lit surface layer of the oceans up to a depth of about 525 feet (160 meters). When the amount of incident sunlight increases in the spring of the year, the phytoplankton begin to flourish.

Like land plants, these tiny microscopic plankton contain chlorophyll and other pigments that capture the sunlight they need for photosynthesis. Photosynthesis transforms solar energy into chemical energy by converting carbon dioxide ($CO_2$) and water ($H_2O$) into molecular oxygen and glucose.

The concentration of phytoplankton in seawater influences the water's ability to reflect sunrays penetrating into the upper layers of the ocean. By measuring the color of the oceans, scientists can determine how much phytoplankton are present in the water. Seawater rich in phytoplankton is blue-green to green in color; cobalt blue waters are aquatic "deserts" – nearly devoid of phytoplankton.

Knowledge of the distribution of phytoplankton is important because the marine food chain begins with phytoplankton's synthesis of organic substances, continues to the zooplankton and the various fishes, and extends all the way up to the giant baleen whales (Bartenwale), which feed exclusively on plankton. Phytoplankton also play an important role as a source of oxygen.

Regions of the ocean that are rich in phosphorus-bearing chemicals (e.g., the subantarctic Atlantic and the waters near the southwestern and northwestern coasts of Africa) also tend to be rich in plankton. Eutrophication of the water due to the growth of plankton is initially useful, but excessive eutrophication can overwhelm and ultimately destroy the region's oxygen supplies. When wastewater interferes with the penetration of sunlight, some forms of plankton cannot survive. Pollution of the oceans discourages the growth of phytoplankton and reduces photosynthesis, which in turn can have negative effects on the production of oxygen.

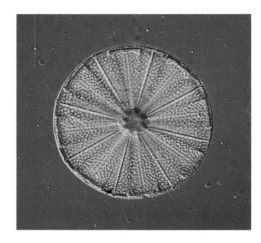

*Phytoplankton are tiny microscopic algae that frequently occur in bizarre shapes. The photo shows the single-celled silicate alga Actinoptychus ondulatus enlarged 300 times.*

## Oceanic Phytoplankton Concentration

Winter

- less than 0.05 milligrams per cubic meter
- 0.05 – 0.10 milligrams per cubic meter
- 0.10 – 0.20 milligrams per cubic meter
- 0.20 – 0.40 milligrams per cubic meter
- 0.40 – 0.60 milligrams per cubic meter
- 0.60 – 0.80 milligrams per cubic meter
- 0.80 – 1.00 milligrams per cubic meter
- 1.00 – 1.50 milligrams per cubic meter
- 1.50 – 2.50 milligrams per cubic meter
- 2.50 – 4.00 milligrams per cubic meter
- 4.00 – 6.00 milligrams per cubic meter
- 6.00 – 10.00 milligrams per cubic meter
- 10.00 – 15.00 milligrams per cubic meter
- 15.00 – 20.00 milligrams per cubic meter
- over 20.00 milligrams per cubic meter
- no available data

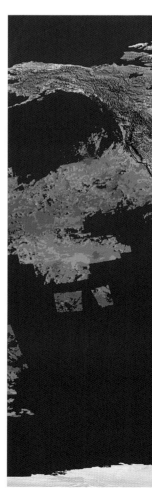

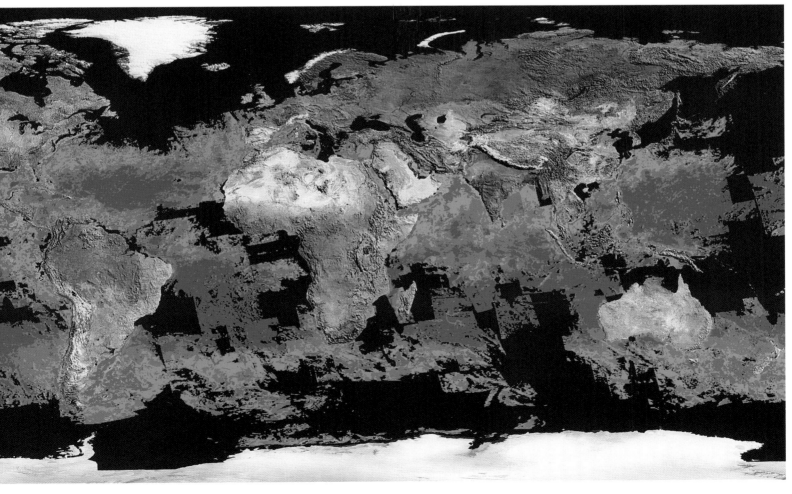

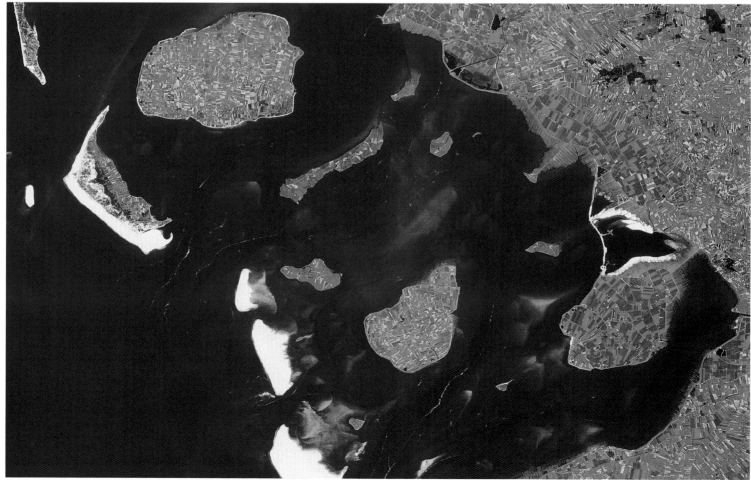

# Ebb and Flood Tides in the Wattenmeer

*The North Frisian island of Amrum (Germany) stretches northward as an elongated sandy hook. Norddorfer Odde Bird Sanctuary is located here. From left to right (east to west), one can see an almost exemplary situation for the Wattenmeer: a narrow marshy edge; higher and partly wooded sandy heathland; then dunes on the North Sea side and a sandy beach.*

Comparing photos taken at various times helps us understand that the Wattenmeer coastline at the North Sea in Germany is subject to continual transformation. Land is continually being destroyed and formed anew. "Watts" (mudflats) form along shallow tidal coasts as amphibious edges between dry land and the open sea. The watt obeys the rhythm of the tides: partly or entirely dry at ebb tide, inundated by seawater at flood tide.

The western boundary of the watt coast is formed by a chain of dune islands with low-lying outer sandbanks that are submerged only during storm floods. These islands include Amrumer Kniepsand, Japsand, Norderoogsand, and Süderoogsand. An unbroken line of dikes delineates the Wattenmeer's eastern boundary. From north to south within the Wattenmeer lie the marshy dike-enclosed islands of Föhr, Langeness, and Pellworm, as well as the inhabited islands of Halligen Gröde, Habel, Hooge, and Nordstrandischmoor, which lie a mere 3.3 to 6.6 feet (one to two meters) above the level of average high tide.

The upper photo on page 86 shows this region at a time when water is low. The network of narrow channels that subdivide the mudflats at low tide is readily visible. These channels begin as shallower or deeper gaps in the outer sandbanks and branch out toward the east. Water from the North Sea

penetrates into the mudflats through these channels. When the tide is ebbing, silt precipitates onto the mudflat and gradually raises its height. During storm floods, the ocean flows through these channels and claims parts of the land for itself.

Catastrophic storm floods called "mandränken" claimed many lives and divided this part of North Frisia into numerous isolated pieces of land in 1364 and 1634. Shortly thereafter, the survivors began building dikes to protect their land and to gain additional land: dike building continues today, although nowadays its purpose is less often to acquire new land than to protect the existing coastline. The outer dike around Hattstedter Marsch (in the center of the picture's eastern edge) was built from 1982 to 1987. This relatively new dike is especially easy to see because it is not yet covered with clover or other vegetation. As part of a project to protect the natural environment, the new polder will include a reservoir basin as well as a number of freshwater and saltwater biotopes.

The other dikes are covered with grass and are therefore only marginally visible in the satellite photo. Pale green to pink in color, their seaward edges feature salt mead-

ows covered with fields of Queller on the silt plains. Toward the land, these two summertime photos reveal clear differences in agricultural patterns. Not yet harvested fields in the fertile marshland appear as dark green patches; pale green color represents meadows and grazing land; reddish tones indicate the settlement patterns of the region, which tend to be either more pointed or elongated in long lines.

National parks with numerous protected reserves have been established along Schleswig-Holstein's tidal coast to protect the extraordinarily rich habitat of the Wattenmeer.

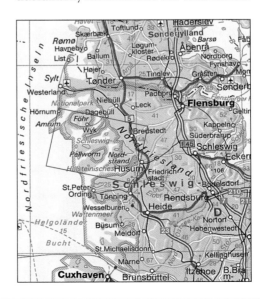

Scale of the map segment: 1 to 2,000,000
0    20    40    60    80    100 km

0         20         40         60         80 Statute
                                            Miles

# A Carpet of Algae in the Adriatic Sea

This satellite photo dates from the summer of 1988 and shows the Italian Adriatic coast from Chioggia in the north to Fano in the south. The Po River delta is readily visible in the northern part of the photo. The waters of the Po carry large amounts of sand, mud, and suspended matter; these materials are deposited offshore, thus gradually extending the coastline farther into the Adriatic. Oxbows in the delta are also readily evident in the photo, which depicts a differential coast with lagoons and sand-

bars. The fine material transported here by the Po is deposited along the coast by wind drift and ocean currents to create a popular sandy beach many miles in length. The central portion of the photo clearly shows the former coastal bays, which have since been severed from the Adriatic to become inland lakes. Apennine foothills are visible in the southwestern corner of the photo. Older cultivated areas are generally smaller than more recently developed fields, many of which are used for growing rice in the Po

multiply explosively in these warm sunlit waters. Fresh breezes from the northeast help to mix and oxygenate them.

The algae coalesce into carpets that drift toward the south, propelled by northeasterly winds and a counterclockwise ocean current. When they drift, they gradually die, as the crimson to orange-red color in the photo shows. In their wake, these dead algae leave behind rotting slime. The putrefaction process robs the water of oxygen needed for the survival of fishes, mol-

*During the 1980s and 1990s, stinking carpets of algae kept many vacationers away from their favorite beaches along the Italian Adriatic. During two consecutive summers, the German automobile club issued weekly reports about the algae situation along the Adriatic's bathing beaches.*

Delta region. Smaller fields are also found among the Apennine foothills.

The most striking features of this satellite photo are the red veils in the otherwise blue waters of the Adriatic. The false-color photo uses reddish shades to depict areas where vegetation is especially active. The veils are dense concentrations of algae floating in the sea. These algae always develop during the summer. The Po River, heavily laden with organic wastes from industry, agriculture, and households, provides nourishment for these algae, which

lusks, and crustaceans, which suffocate as a result.

Another consequence of the algae plague that struck this region during the 1980s and 1990s is a decline in tourism by more than 40 percent along the sandy coast between Venice and Ancona. The Italian government instituted a series of emergency programs, which include the construction of sewage treatment plants and a reduction in the amount of chemicals used in agriculture. The effort to combat pollution in the Po River, however, will take decades, since nearly all of the wastewater from the highly industrialized regions and intensively cultivated fields of northern Italy is poured into this river.

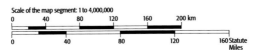

Scale of the map segment: 1 to 4,000,000

0    40    80    120    160    200 km

0    40    80    120    160 Statute Miles

# The Ocean Currents

**Ocean Currents**

- warm current
- cold current

**Speed of the Current**

- 6 – 12 nautical miles in 24 hours
- 12 – 24 nautical miles in 24 hours
- more than 24 nautical miles in 24 hours
- 6 – 12 nautical miles in 24 hours
- 12 – 24 nautical miles in 24 hours

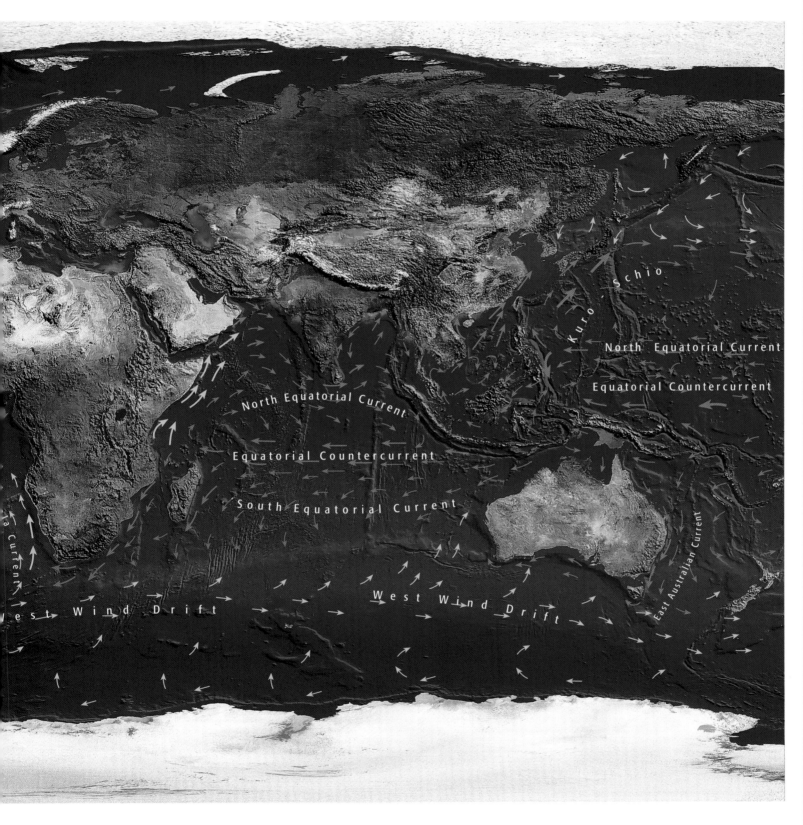

The planetary wind system causes two large-scale whirls to form in the Atlantic Ocean and two similar vortices to arise in the Pacific Ocean. The Equatorial Countercurrent separates the two in the Pacific. Their eastern branches, propelled by off-shore winds, are composed of cold, rising water. Because of the shape of its coastline, South America deflects the Atlantic's South Equatorial Current northward and increases the strength of the Gulf Stream, which penetrates as far north as the Arctic. Currents in the northern part of the Indian Ocean change direction annually in accordance with the rhythm of the monsoons.

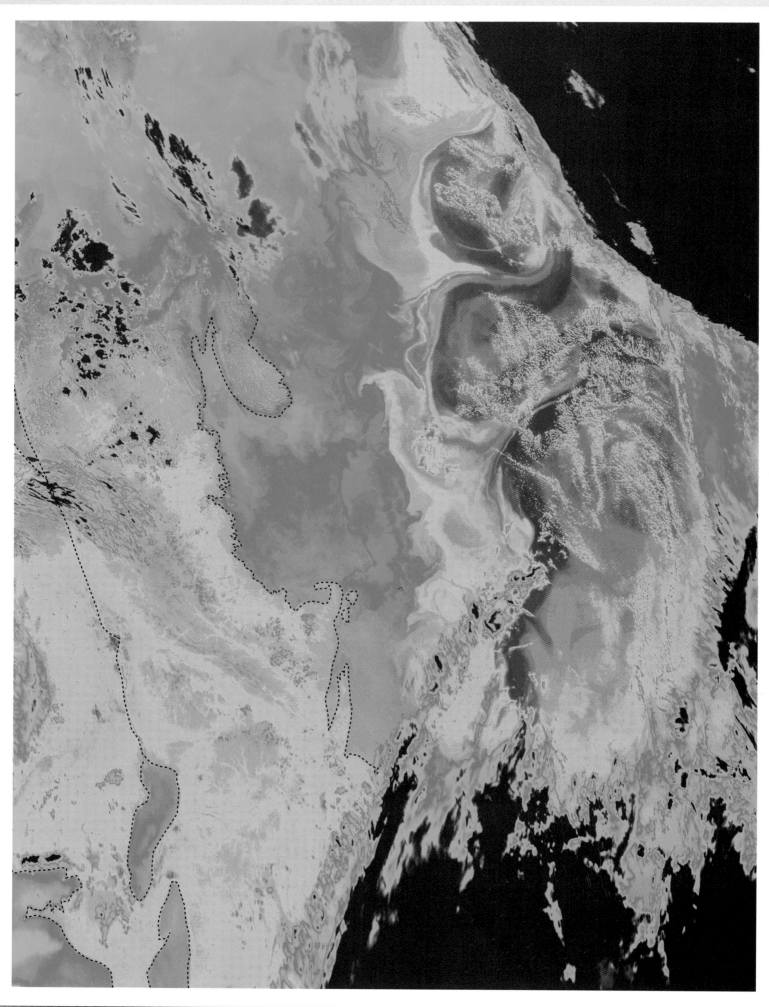

# The Gulf Stream

This colorful satellite photograph is a so-called "thermal image" depicting variations in temperature as different shades of color. The part of the photograph that has not been distorted shows the Gulf Stream off the eastern coast of North America. Orientation points include parts of Lake Erie (visible as green patches in the lower left corner) and Lake Huron, and the entirety of Lake Ontario, with the Saint Lawrence River flowing toward the northeast like a slender green thread. As a boundary between yellowish and greenish hues, dotted lines coincide with the Atlantic coastline from elongated Long Island (in New York State), across Cape Cod (near Boston), and northeastward to Nova Scotia. The confusing dark blue patches, especially in the lower and upper right-hand corners of the photo, are caused by high-altitude clouds and veils of clouds. This photo was taken during the night, which explains why the continent appears relatively cool (yellow).

The Gulf Stream itself is clearly visible in the center of the photo as an area of red, orange, and yellow tones. These colors indicate warmer temperatures. The arc-shaped structures within this area represent vortices of warmer water along transition zones with cooler water masses.

The so-called Gulf Stream is actually a system of ocean currents: complex exchange processes draw warm water from the tropical Caribbean Sea and Gulf of Mexico northeastward along the North American coast and carry that water across the Atlantic and toward Europe's western and northern Atlantic coasts. The system is fed from two sources: one part of the water comes from the North Equatorial Current;

the other part from the South Equatorial Current. Together with the Antilles Current, the aforementioned currents join to create the Gulf Stream, which (along the eastern side of the Atlantic) is known as the Gulf Stream Drift or Atlantic Current. The Gulf Stream system, which carries tremendous masses of water and vast amounts of energy, is propelled by the following "motors." One source of propulsion comes from the trade winds, which cause warm surface water to drift westward, where it is deflected to the north and south by North America's eastern coast. As it travels north or south, some of this water evaporates. It cools and some of it freezes at higher latitudes, which increases the relative salinity of the remaining water. Both processes cause increases in the density of the surface water, which (as heavy North Atlantic water) sinks down and (much like an old-fashioned paternoster elevator) draws more surface water from the Caribbean. In this way, some 600 million cubic feet (17 million cubic meters) of water descend into the North Atlantic every second. Because of its enormously long north-south axis, the Atlantic has the strongest longitudinal circulation of all the world's oceans. It is connected to all the other oceans like a flow-through heater. The following example will help elucidate just how much energy is actually stored in the water: if the air in the Arctic is 36 degrees Fahrenheit (20 degrees Celsius) colder than the Gulf Stream's water surface, an area of ocean 3.9 square miles (10 square kilometers) in size yields as

much energy as is produced by all of Germany's atomic power plants. Cold, deep-flowing water flows back around the southern tip of Africa and into the northern Pacific, where it rises along the western coast of North America and returns to its original location in a pattern of global water circulation. It takes about 1,000 years to complete one such cycle.

The efficiency of this "aqueous elevator" is strongly dependent upon the salinity of the surface water. Salinity, in turn, is determined by global climatic developments. Global warming melts inland ice, which reduces the relative salinity of the oceans and can cause the "heat pump" to run more slowly, to shift toward the south, or to quit pumping entirely. Changes in oceanic circulation can have devastating effects on the planet's climate. A computer simulation based on a global warming of just 5.4 degrees Fahrenheit (3 degrees Celsius) would drastically reduce temperatures in Europe and North America because it would stop the Gulf Stream from carrying warm water to the north and east. Northern Europe would disappear under a blanket of ice; icebergs would penetrate as far south as the Canary Islands. Extensive white ice surfaces would reflect incident solar radiation almost completely, and this would cause still further reductions in temperature. It would seem that interference with the oceanic "elevator" could cause the return of an Ice Age. According to the most recent research, the transition from a warm period to a cold period can occur in just a few decades. Stopping the "warm pump" would also mean that $CO_2$ (the "greenhouse gas") derived from the atmosphere would no longer be temporarily stored in the ocean's depths, but would be available to further accelerate planetary warming.

*Narvik, in northern Norway, has an ice-free harbor throughout the year. Inuvik, Canada, which is located at a comparable latitude, experiences January temperatures of minus 22 degrees Fahrenheit (minus 30 degrees Celsius). The Gulf Stream, which carries warm water to western and northern Europe, is responsible for the positive temperature anomalies that occur along the Norwegian coast.*

Scale of the map segment: 1 to 80,000,000

| 0 | 800 | 1600 | 2400 | 3200 | 4000 km |

| 0 | 800 | 1600 | 2400 | 3000 |
Statute Miles

# Agrarian Colonization in Rondonia, Brazil

"We must conquer our land, possess our earth, march towards the west...." With this proclamation, former Brazilian president Juscelino Kubitschek launched one of the planet's largest settlement programs. Although the measures are gargantuan in scale, open to public scrutiny, and responsible for enormous environmental changes, they nonetheless evoke far less public interest than the settlement of the North American West, a project that has long since been relegated to the history books.

Until the mid-1970s, the intrusion of stock-raising operations into formerly mostly untouched areas was the principal cause of massive environmental destruction in the Brazilian Amazon and in Latin America as a whole. Valuable ecosystems that had taken centuries or millennia to evolve fell – and are still falling victim – to the myopic greediness for short-term profits by privileged individual entrepreneurs and national or international agribusinesses. Job creation has generally been quite limited: Brazil's huge ranches employ only one human worker for every 3,000 head of cattle.

There are many private and public motives for the settlement of the Brazilian Amazonian lowland and the western edge of Brazil. Underprivileged peoples in the extremely impoverished rural regions of northeastern and southern Brazil hope to find a chance for survival in the rain forest regions. The state regards the planned or spontaneous agricultural colonization as a safety valve that reduces social tensions and provides a cheap alternative to urgently needed agrarian reforms. Finally, it is hoped that the exploitation of the region's

incalculable trove of natural resources will not only help modernize regional industries but will also increase the wealth of the nation as a whole.

After the abominable failure of colonization attempts in the Amazonian lowlands per se and especially along the Transamazônica, since the early 1980s efforts have focused on the federal state of Rondonia. Once a peripheral boundary land between the federal states of Amazonas in the north and Mato Grosso in the east, Rondonia is currently experiencing the fastest population growth in the entire country. Home to a mere 111,000 people in 1971, Rondonia's population had quadrupled by 1991. Nevertheless, with an average of only about 13 inhabitants per square mile (five inhabitants per square kilometer), Rondonia is still very sparsely inhabited and seems able to accept a virtually unlimited number of newcomers.

In fact, the greater portion of Rondonia, which lies outside the Amazon Basin and within the perennially moist tropics, offers more favorable natural conditions for development than the Amazon lowlands themselves. The climate in the tablelands of the Brazilian Shield, which is divided into gentle ridges and broad planes, features a three-month-long dry season that lasts from June to August. Because of the intermittent availability of moisture, the region's forests are no longer tropical rain forest, but occur as transitional forms that lose their leaves during dry periods or as bush forests in the Cerrado Formation at higher elevations. As aridity increases toward the south, natural grassy savannas (campos cerrados) appear with greater frequency. Fertile pod-

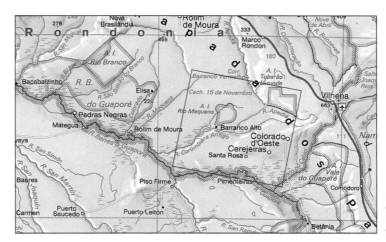

Scale of the map segment: 1 to 4,000,000

sols increasingly replace the sterile latosols of the Amazonian lowlands. Better soil offers the possibility of developing permanent agricultural and grazing lands.

Along with more fertile soils and richer bodies of water, experiences gained during the failed projects that attempted to colonize the Amazon region provided valuable lessons for this second generation of agricultural colonization in Brazil. State coordination and support were better, if not optimal, and immigrants from central and southern Brazil were more likely to bring agricultural skills and even a modicum of capital along with them. A greater percentage of work-intensive and care-intensive tree and bush plantations, especially cocoa and coffee plantations, were planned from the start, and this helped to minimize the risks associated with cultivation. Nowa-

days, Rondonia is not only autonomous in food production, but actually harvests significant surpluses.

The satellite photo (pp. 104–105) shows a segment of extreme southerly Rondonia with the boundary river Guaporé (at the southern edge of the photo) that demarcates the border with Bolivia. This region is somewhat afield of the central axis of development, which follows the famous federal route 364 from Cuiaba to Porto Velho. Three very dissimilar structures are clearly visible.

Extensive grazing lands, which belong to traditionally large-scale operations and often exceed 250,000 acres (100,000 hectares) in area, fill the river valleys along Rio Corumbiara Antigo. These grasslands are connected to distant urban centers by a sparse network of unpaved roads and rural

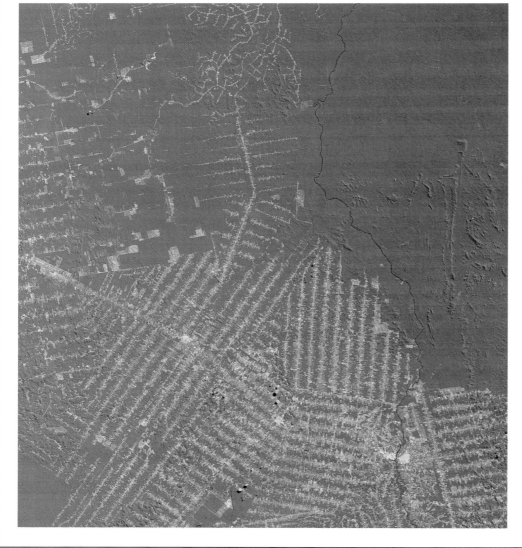

tracks. In low-lying areas, recurrent flooding by mineral-rich, sediment-rich waters from the region's rivers deposits natural fertilizers. In addition, and especially at the end of the dry season, large expanses of these grazing lands are set afire. Burnt-over areas appear as dark red patches on the satellite photo.

The Colorado d'Oeste colonization region adjoins toward the east. This project, one of the oldest in Rondonia, was carried out between 1970 and 1981 with large contributions from the World Bank. It shows the typical settlement pattern of clearly planned main and secondary axes with adjacent, elongated, agricultural plots measuring 250 acres (100 hectares) each. The forests are cleared successively, beginning near the road, and a corridor of forest is supposed to be left standing between the strips. Planned intermediate settlements (Nucleo Urbano) are built at major intersections. These nuclei are equipped with publicly accessible infrastructure and state-run storehouses. After land was abandoned by small farmers and subsequently purchased by groups with more capital at their disposal, a

number of scattered large-scale farming operations arose in this zone.

A more recent colonization region, which adjoins this one to the northwest, has been deliberately reserved for latifundia. These large, landed estates own at least several thousand acres and generally conduct intensive cattle-raising operations. Here too, meadows are routinely set afire. In order to make a fast profit, landowners often sow African grasses on the cleared areas. But the productivity of these artificially cultivated meadows declines sharply after a few years have passed. Other problems, including increased erosion, exacerbate the degradation of the soil. It is not atypical to find massive intervention in Brazil's natural landscape, even in regions that should be preserved intact as taboo zones, for example, within the Rio Mequens Indian Reservation.

*The difference between natural forests, which are home to a wide diversity of species, and degraded areas couldn't be more obvious. Only a few fire-resistant trees have survived on the burnt-over area. The cleared land is quickly colonized by low-quality grasses whose productivity rapidly decreases within a few years' time due to desiccation and lack of nutrients.*

*Unpaved roads through the rain forest facilitate its settlement – and its destruction. They are often first built only as logging roads, but (because of the enormous population pressure) soon provide access for settlers who penetrate from the road into forest with neither plans nor permission.*

# Clear-cuts in Russia's Taiga

The area shown in the satellite photo is located about 600 miles (1,000 kilometers) north-northeast of Moscow and about 250 miles (400 kilometers) east of Archangelsk, far from regional railway lines and roads. It belongs to the autonomous republic of the Komi, a people who traditionally make their living from hunting, fishing, and forestry. With fewer than 26 inhabitants per square mile (10 inhabitants per square kilometer), the region as a whole is sparsely settled. Settlements are visible only in the plant-free areas along the southern edge of the photo.

From its headwaters along the flanks of Timan Ridge, the Mezen River flows in a mighty curve as it crosses the gently rolling and in parts marshy taiga west of the Ural Mountains, before it empties into the White Sea at Mezen Bay. Because of the cool and moist continental climate in the "Far North" of European Russia, the river is iced over from late October until mid-May and is only navigable this far inland during the spring. Temperatures can fall below minus 58 degrees Fahrenheit (minus 50 degrees Celsius) during the region's extremely cold winters, which generally last from 180 to 220 days.

Ever since people first settled here, the region's enormous boreal coniferous forests (together with fishing and hunting) have formed the basis of the region's economy. Inclement climate and permafrost preclude agricultural use of the soil; seasonal insect plagues exacerbate the harshness of life in this region.

What this photo so clearly reveals are open wounds in the landscape caused by the

*This block hut is located in northern Russia, far from any form of civilization. This is the transition zone between the closed forest of the taiga region and the forested tundra. Along with coniferous trees, birches and small-leafed bushes also grow here.*

ruthless exploitation of nature. Almost all of the forests along the curve of the Mezen River have been completely clear-cut. The devastation proceeds according to plan along arrow-straight logging roads. Most of these roads end at the Mezen or its tributaries, where the logs are unloaded into the rivers and floated downstream to wood-processing industrial plants along the coast. The exploitation began during the Stalinist era, especially after the Second World War. At first, and continuing through the 1950s, labor costs were kept to a minimum because the workers were either prisoners of war or forced laborers. Afterwards, these laborers were replaced by work brigades from the Komsomol and by soldiers.

Russia's taiga comprises about half of the Earth's coniferous forests. About one-third of the forested area is currently being exploited for the wood-products industry by Russian or foreign companies. According to the International Forestry Institute in Moscow, wastage amounts to between 20 and 40 percent because cut trees either rot on site or sink into the rivers during transport. Obsolete logging techniques cause additional, nearly irreparable damage to the landscape. The delicate soil of the taiga is so severely damaged that no trees can grow again for a long time; reforestation is often ignored because it reduces short-term profits.

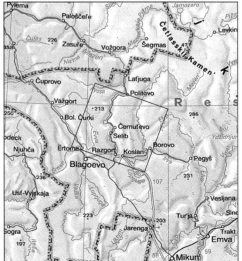

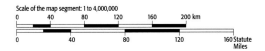

Scale of the map segment: 1 to 4,000,000

0   40   80   120   160   200 km

0            40            80            120            160 Statute Miles

# Forest Fires in Manchuria

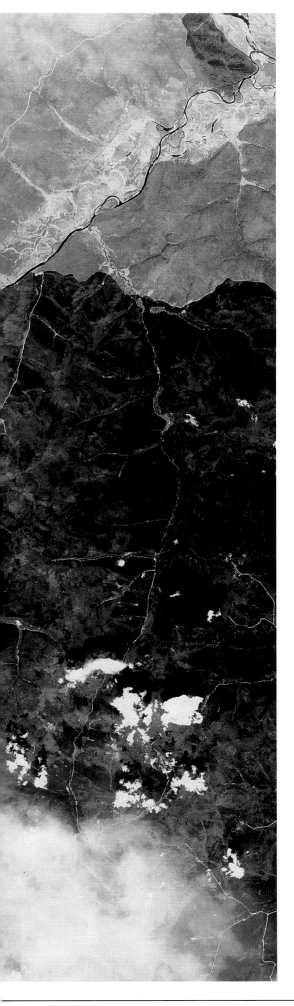

In extreme northern China, in the province of Heilongjiang, a forest fire raged for more than three weeks in May 1987, before it could finally be extinguished. More than 200 people died in the blaze; 50,000 were left homeless; and the regional capital of Mohe (Xilinji) burned to the ground. Official reports about the extent of the burnt area varied from 2,200 to more than 3,800 square miles (5,800 to 10,000 square kilometers). Five forest workers were arrested and convicted of having caused the blaze through what Chinese authorities described as "neglect of their duties." Because authorities initially underestimated the severity of the threat, it took a long time before the fire could finally be brought under control. Local administrators were also convicted of negligence; after expressing self-criticism, even the forestry minister was ousted.

Enormous forest fires burn near the northern and southern edges of the photo; gigantic burnt-over areas fill the center of the photo. The blackened color of this latter area contrasts with the pale lines of logging roads. The Emuerhe, a right-hand tributary of the Amur River, is readily visible as a meandering line. This hilly region with its wide valleys belongs to the northern foothills of the Great Xingan (Chingan). Elevations in this low-mountain region range from 1,000 to 2,000 feet (300 to 600 meters). One of China's most densely forested areas, the region provides raw materials for major paper and wood-processing industries.

The reason forest fires recur here so often is related to the composition of these forests, the low humidity of the air, the dryness of the wood, and certain climatic factors. Winters are long, cold, and dry; summers are brief and hot with great variations in the amount of precipitation. During the spring, when the larch, birch, and poplar forests are dry, it takes only a mild breeze and a few sparks to kindle a running fire on the ground or a crown fire in the tops of the trees. Winds in this region are especially strong during the springtime. Fortunately, the 1987 fires did not create a total catastrophe because the soil at higher elevations had not yet thawed. This protected the roots of many deciduous trees from being killed in the blaze.

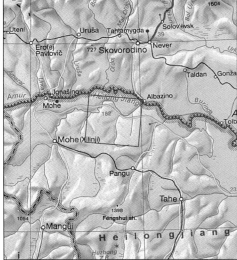

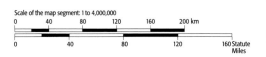

*Larch forests are an important natural resource in northern Manchuria. These trees are especially vulnerable to fire because their bark contains flammable resins and because their crowns are extremely dry and readily combustible during the springtime.*

Scale of the map segment: 1 to 4,000,000

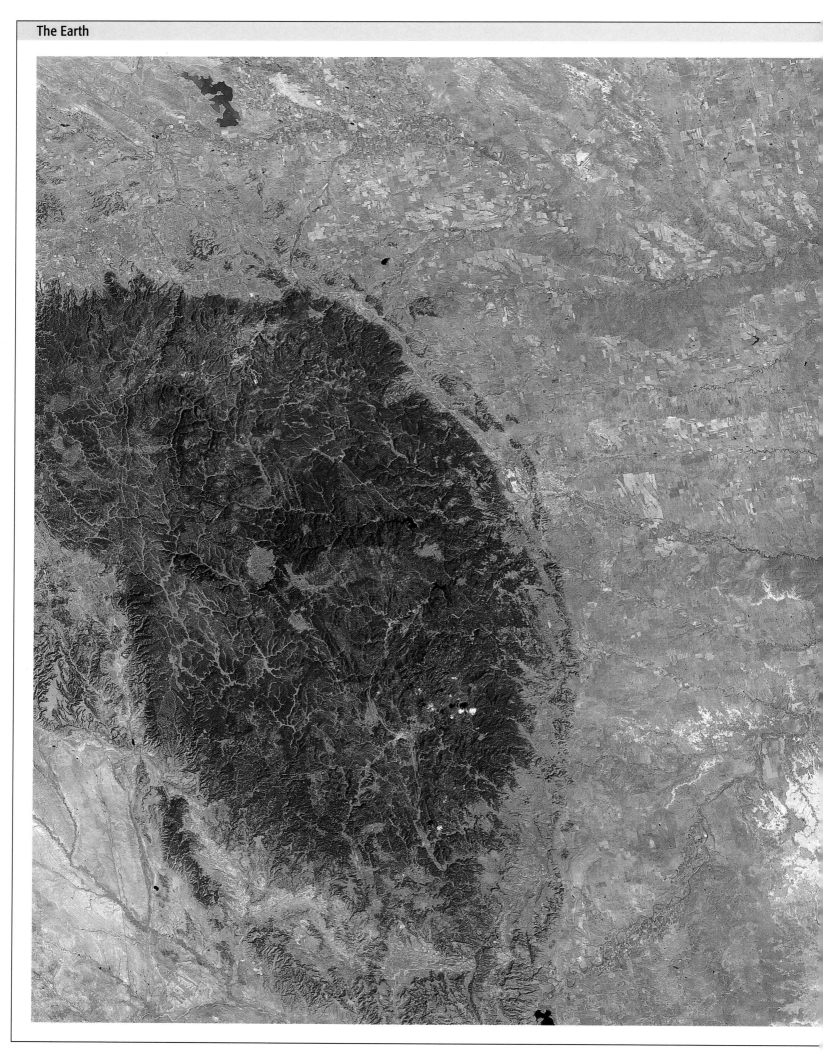

# Soil Erosion in the Badlands

*As if this were a lunar landscape, one gazes across the fields on the high ground, across an eroded ravine, and into the Badlands of South Dakota. In the background, parts of the serrated older plain have already been eroded entirely.*

On the one hand, a tourist attraction; on the other hand, an example of soil degradation: the Badlands in the United States are a fascinating landscape and a warning about what can happen when nature is ruthlessly exploited.

The satellite photo shows a segment of the northern Great Plains, the flat, gently eastward-sloping plain to the east of the North American cordilleras. The Black Hills, a forest-covered mountainous area below the Rocky Mountains, are easily distinguished. The Great Plains are prairie lands, formerly the habitat of vast herds of buffalo. An open and nearly treeless grassland, this region is especially suitable for large-scale pastoral farming. As the settlement of America progressed from east to west, agriculture penetrated progressively farther westward, indigenous peoples were displaced, and pastoral farming was concentrated within smaller areas. Agriculture was conducted in regions of extremely variable precipitation, which meant that harvests were likewise unreliable. Farming removed the original plant cover and exposed topsoil to high velocity winds, which soon carried off vast quantities of valuable soil. Heavy rains fell on naked, bone-dry soil, causing linear and planar erosion. Ravine-shaped erosion channels (called "gullies" in America) ate their way upward into the watersheds of rivers and brooks; in the course of several decades, huge areas of land were eroded to depths ranging from one story to as much as 490 feet (150 meters);

billions of tons of fertile soil were washed southward into the Gulf of Mexico. Nearly half a million farmers were compelled to abandon their farms.

The satellite photo shows the patchwork pattern of farms that resulted from American surveying methods. The lush vegetation in the river valleys that descend eastward toward the Mississippi River contrasts vividly with the dryness of this region, which lies in the rain shadow of the cordilleras to the west. Readily visible in the photo is the feather-like pattern that results when gully erosion extends upward from rivers into farmed fields. In the southeastern corner of the photo, erosion has exposed a paler layer of soil, which forms a temporary base. The rivers draining this area are white because of the pale color of suspended sediments. Remnants of older farmed fields rise above the surrounding land.

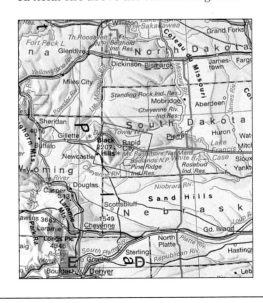

Scale of the map segment: 1 to 12,000,000

0    120    240    360    480    600 km

0    120    240    360    480
Statute Miles

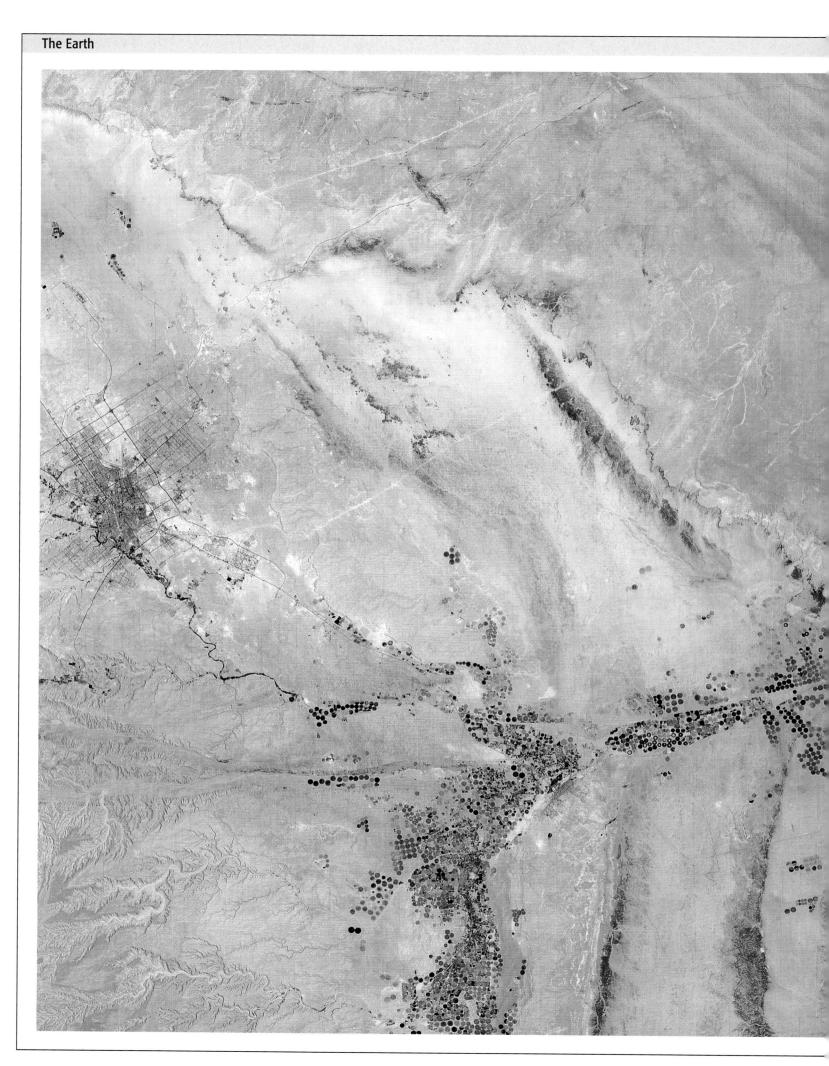

# Irrigation in Saudi Arabia

*Computerized self-piloting sprinkler systems rotate around their supply line and dispense valuable, irreplaceable water pumped from ancient reserves some 100 to 920 feet (30 to 280 meters) below the flat, sandy surface. Rows of trees have been planted to try to slow or stop the advance of the dunes.*

Green disks lie atop the yellow sand like confetti strewn across the broad expanse of the desert. Automated mobile sprinkler systems pump low-lying groundwater to the surface and irrigate the desert sands of Saudi Arabia.

The satellite photo shows the southeastern vicinity of Ar-Riyad (Riyadh), the capital city of Saudi Arabia. The Nedjed Plateau with Ar-Riyad is a crossroads and serves as the link between the northern nomadic way of life, oasis farming in the south, oil production in the Arabian Gulf, and religious centers (Mecca and Medina) on the Red Sea.

Reddish-brown colored stripes in the photo represent stepped sedimentary ridges composed of layers of limestone that have reached the surface. White fields of sand stretch between them and sometimes grow together to form densely dune-covered areas, as is the case at the eastern edge of the

photo. The moderately steep, stepped sedimentary hillsides in the western part of the photo display the characteristic feather-like patterns of erosive ravines, which are only seldom filled with water. These wadis drain into the fields of dunes, where their water is absorbed by the thirsty sand.

The old oasis called al-Harg appears in the picture as an inconspicuous area with many small dots. Old oases like this one produce a variety of crops: dates, vegetables, dye and feed plants, and a few varieties of grain. The new irrigated area, which was built during the 1980s, shows a clear structure: it stretches eastward from the mountainous region along a sandy valley toward the dunes. Dark disks represent areas that were under irrigation at the time this photo was taken; yellowish disks are either covered with sere plants and lying fallow or have been abandoned, as have many fields on the northern edge between al-Harg and Ar-Riyad.

Wealthy Saudi Arabia compensates for its scarcity of precipitation by drilling wells and desalinating seawater. Thanks to the construction of new irrigation systems, the country has specialized in the cultivation of wheat and feed crops and has become the world's sixth largest wheat exporter. But the groundwater used to irrigate these crops is "fossil water" deposited about 20,000 years ago during a moister climatic period. About 1,000 quarts of nonrenewable water are expended to produce each pound of Saudi wheat (2,000 liters per kilogram).

Scale of the map segment: 1 to 4,000,000

0    40    80    120    160    200 km

0         40         80         120      160 Statute Miles

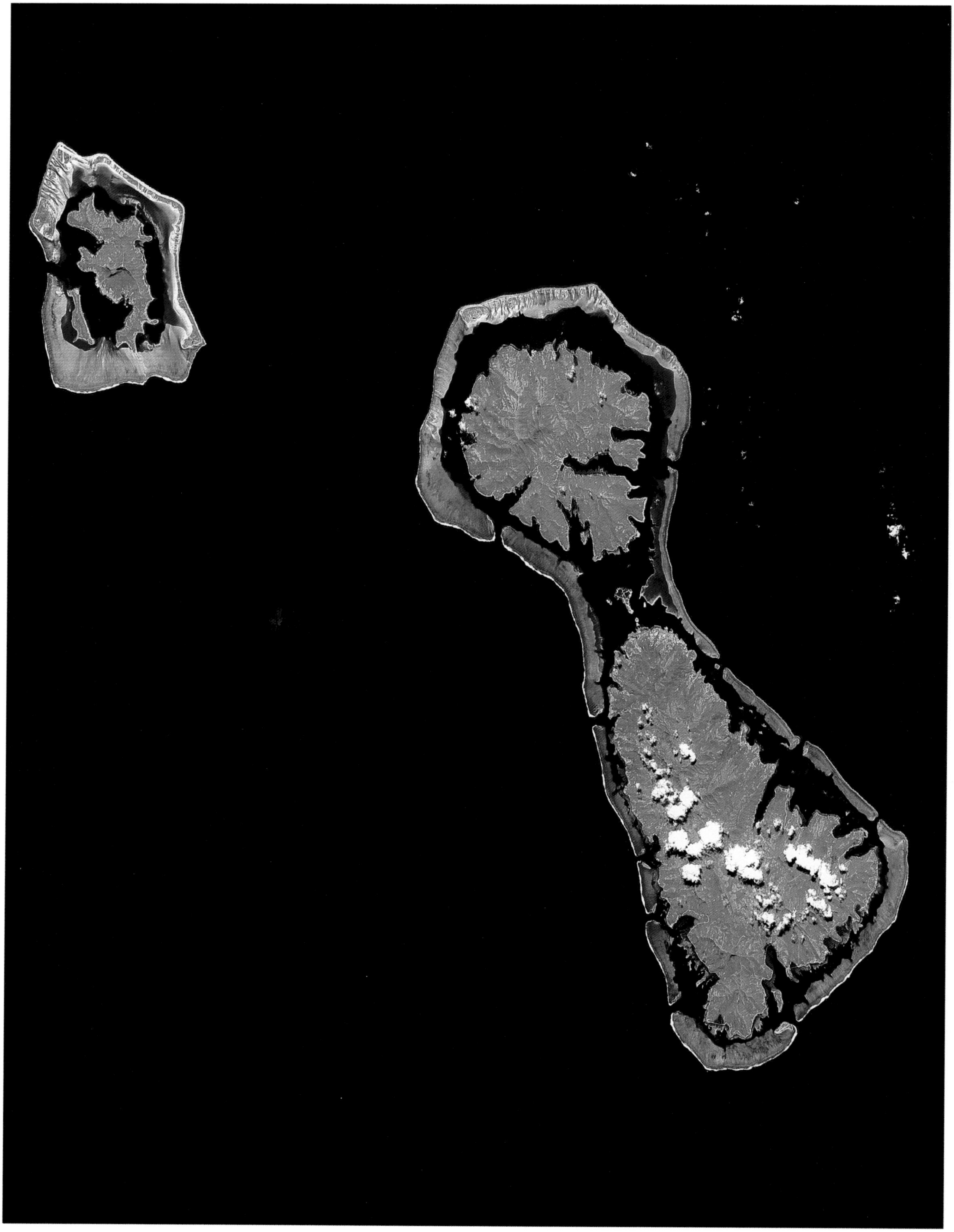

# Endangered Coral Reefs

Coral reefs, like thin eggshells, surround the tropical green islands of the Society Islands in the South Pacific Ocean. Tahiti is the best-known island in this group. But what looks at first glance like the eternal dream of an island paradise is actually an extremely fragile ecosystem.

Many islands in the tropics are surrounded by a more or less continuous ring of coral reefs, which sometimes emerge from the ocean to form wreath-like chains of low-lying islands.

Islands of this kind develop only in clear, oxygen-rich, high-salinity seawater whose monthly average minimum temperature does not drop below 71.6 degrees Fahrenheit (22 degrees Celsius) and whose absolute minimum temperature is not less than 64.4 degrees Fahrenheit (18 degrees Celsius). Only under such conditions can coral polyps survive and filter calcium carbonate from the seawater to build their fragile chalky skeletons. These skeletons are subsequently colonized by algae, which fill the hollow spaces and solidify and cement the skeletons.

The characteristic ring shape of coral reefs around tropical islands often begins as a reef attached to slowly subsiding volcanic mountains. If the volcano sinks below sea level, an atoll is formed consisting solely of the wreath-shaped reef. The interior of the reef (as in this satellite photo) is usually a rather shallow lagoon seldom more than a few dozen yards (a few dozen meters) deep, but its seaward slope usually declines steeply, often to depths of several thousand yards (meters) below the sea. Since coral thrives best along the outer edge of the ring, the interior lagoon gradually fills with dead coral branches and parts of branches.

Coral reefs, and especially atolls, are severely endangered. The complex symbiosis within such reefs cannot tolerate rapid and drastic changes in living conditions. A sudden rise in sea level, which is to be feared in the wake of global warming, would submerge the coral too quickly to depths where they could no longer survive. Their death would also mean the demise of entire nations – like the Maldives or certain nations in Micronesia – because these countries rely on coral reefs to protect their islands, which often lie only a very few meters above sea level, from tidal flooding. Pollutants in the oceans, especially crude oil, stick to the coral and reduce the translucency of the seawater. Effluents from coastal industries, which frequently have high concentrations of heavy metals and a tendency to deoxygenate their surroundings, poison the coral polyps. Airports, har-

*The double summits of Bora-Bora Island tower above a surrounding reef that protects many small islands within the turquoise-blue waters of an extensive lagoon. As is the case among many South Pacific islands, an extinct volcano forms the core of the island. Only the hard basalt of its volcanic chimney has resisted erosion.*

bor buildings, and hotels are often built from chalky coral blocks quarried from the reefs. The removal of this material creates entirely new currents along the reef and in the lagoon. Sport divers hunting for underwater souvenirs and improperly anchored boats can damage parts of the delicate reef and thus also destroy the beauty of their favorite diving areas. Last but by no means least, atomic testing in the South Seas has caused severe vibrations in the reef structures whose effects sometimes do not manifest themselves for many years.

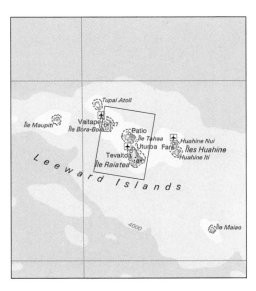

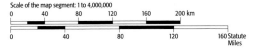

Scale of the map segment: 1 to 4,000,000

0   40   80   120   160   200 km

0   40   80   120   160 Statute Miles

117

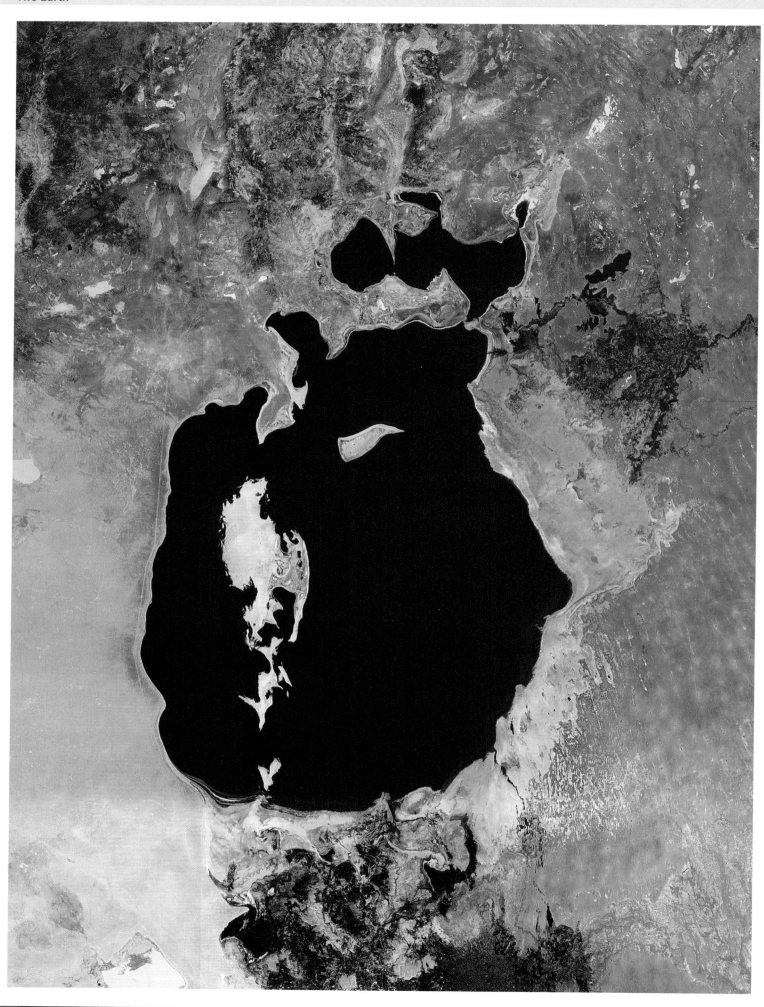

# The Silting Up of the Aral Sea

In the Turan lowlands of central Asia, in Kazakhstan and Uzbekistan, between the Kara Kum and Kysyl deserts in the east and the hilly and mountainous lands of the Ustjurt Plateau in the west, lies the heavily saline Aral Sea. The world's fourth-largest inland lake, which has no outlet, is fed by waters carried here by the Amudarija and Syrdarija Rivers. Salt lakes, salt crusts, salt swamps, flats of salty clay where lakes have dried up, sandy planes, and inland dunes all testify to the desertlike character of this region.

Until a few decades ago, countless small bays and sandy offshore islands dotted the Aral Sea's flat eastern and southern shores. These shores differed markedly from the steep western shore, whose elevation was more than 330 feet (100 meters) higher. Today, this difference in elevation has been nearly eradicated. As late as the 1960s, the fishing town of Mujnok still lay on the Aral Sea's southern shore and a ferry route linked it with Aralsk on the northern shore. Nowadays, the shoreline has retreated 22 miles (36 kilometers) from the settlement.

Within a mere 30 years' time, the Aral Sea has lost more than half its area (1960: 26,800 square miles = 69,500 square kilometers; 1992: 13,000 square miles = 33,600 square kilometers) and two-thirds of its volume. The elevation of the lake's surface has declined 54.1 feet (16.5 meters). Islands united with the surrounding land, severing the northern part of the lake, and new islands emerged. The lake's salinity increased from 5 grams per liter to 30 grams per liter. Storms whirl up between 83 and 110 million short tons (75 and 100 million metric tons) of salt and dust from the exposed plain each year.

What has caused these drastic changes?

Neither the deposition of sediments, the growth of plants, nor human efforts to gain more dry land have caused this body of water to dry up. The Aral Sea has shrunk because nine-tenths of the water flowing in its tributary rivers, is diverted to irrigate cotton fields, fruit plantations, and fields of grapes and tobacco. Three times more water evaporates from the lake than is carried into it by its tributaries to replace the loss. As part of the socialist Soviet Union's centrally administrated economic planning, agricultural cultivation in this arid region has increased from 6.9 to nearly 20 million acres (from 2.8 to nearly 8 million hectares) since the 1960s. Groundwater levels have decreased and the soil has become progressively more salty, two factors that reduce the productivity of cultivated fields (which appear as red patches in

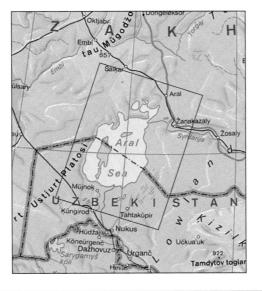

the satellite photos) in the lower reaches and deltas of the Amudarija and Syrdarija. Today, the small volume of water is permitted to reach the Aral Sea is extremely salty and severely polluted.

*A comparison of these two satellite photos — one taken in the 1970s, the other in the 1980s — reveals the drastic changes in the size of the Aral Sea, which was once famous for its freshwater fauna, which included sturgeon, carp, Barben and Hausen. Today, 20 of its former 24 species of fish have disappeared and the fisheries industry is dead. Every year, winds deposit 10 short tons of salt onto each acre of soil (4 metric tons per hectare). Salt deposition is gradually destroying the fertility of the thick layer of humus.*

Scale of the map segment: 1 to 12,000,000

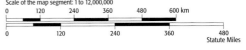

# Urban Metropolis: Mexico City

More extensively than in any other country on Earth, Mexico's newspapers print daily and highly detailed reports on air-pollution levels in Mexico City, the national capital. Our planet's largest urban population center continues to expand under the sharp and steady pressure of immigration. About 2,000 newcomers arrive each day from rural areas in this Central American country. Along with a large number of unemployed and underemployed people, child laborers (especially on the streets) are a typical sight. About 16 million of Mexico's 93 million people currently live in the capital, whose "Zona Metropolitana" includes the central capital "Mexico D. F." and 33 surrounding communities.

Mexico City's high valley, visible at the northern edge of the satellite photo, stretches across the central Mexican highlands, an area rich in geographic and geological contrasts. The concentration of people and industry makes it the core region of the entire nation. Numerous ash cones and volcanoes tower above the valley; the tallest and best-known peak is the 17,930-foot (5,465-meter) Popocatepetl, visible at the eastern edge of the photo. A moderately warm climate with dry winters predominates in this transitional area between temperate and cold zones (tierra templada and tierra fria).

Mexico City is bursting its seams, especially in the northwest, where it is expanding onto the bed of formerly extensive but now mostly dry Lake Texcoco. The remnants of that lake are readily apparent in the photo.

*Temperature inversions occur on more than 200 days each year, increasing the concentration of airborne toxins and suffocating Mexico City and its high surrounding valley under a foul blanket of polluted air.*

The Mexican capital thrived during the long incumbency (1877–1911) of the dictator Díaz, who conducted aggressive policies of development and modernization. Two-thirds of Mexico's industrial production is currently concentrated in the vicinity of the capital city and in the Monterrey area in the federal state of Nuevo León. Administration and commerce were somewhat decentralized after the severe 1985 earthquake; since then, construction of new industrial sites has not been permitted in Mexico Federal District. This restriction is intended to ease the strains on an environment, which is becoming increasingly unbearable for its 15 million people. At altitudes ranging from 7,200 to 7,550 feet (2,200 to 2,300 meters), the burdens placed on the atmosphere, vegetation, soil, and water systems threaten to exceed the limits of nature's regenerative capacities.

At these high altitudes, intense ultraviolet radiation reacts with emissions from more than 40,000 industrial sites and millions of motor vehicles to create severe photochemical smog. International pollution limits are frequently exceeded, which causes an unduly high frequency of bronchial ailments, conjunctivitis, and infections of the mucous membranes. Human activities increase the temperature of the air near the ground by 7 to 9 degrees Fahrenheit (4 to 5 degrees Celsius): this climate can now only theoretically be described as "cool temperate," and the natural ventilation of this high valley is no longer adequate. In the past, air pollution has been exacerbated by dust storms that ensued when the lake bottom dried out. The situation gradually improves during rainy seasons thanks to the so-called "wash-out" effect.

Declining groundwater levels have made water scarce; its costly transport from increasingly distant sources in the mountains or from lowland sources near the ocean has become unavoidable. The sewage system serves only about half of the city's population and releases mostly untreated wastewater into the northern canals and rivers. This causes pollution whose effects are felt as far away as the rivers' mouth zones in the Gulf of Mexico.

There is serious reason to doubt that the decentralization concept will actually lead to decreased immigration and to improvements in the traffic, supply, and environmental problems. Even the urban population's understandable wish to escape on weekends from the hell of the inner city only creates additional environmental problems.

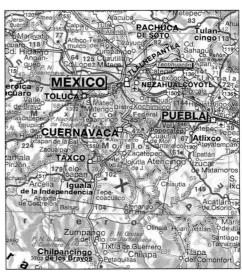

Scale of the map segment: 1 to 4,000,000

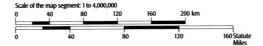

# Europe from Space

## Topographic Forms

- high mountains
- moderately high mountains
- lowland
- fault zone
- skerry
- fjord
- lagoon
- river delta
- glacier
- island
- peninsula

Europe is essentially an extreme westerly peninsula of the Eurasian continent. Its eastern boundary is drawn along a line from the Ural Mountains, along the Ural River and the northern edge of the Caucasus Mountains, through the Black Sea, the Bosporus, the Sea of Marmara and the Dardanelles, and into the Aegean Sea.

Europe is the world's most subdivided continent. Islands and peninsulas comprise more than one-third of its 390,000-million-square-mile (10-million-square-kilometer) area, which explains why its coastline is more than 23,000 (37,000 kilometers) long. The average distance from a seacoast is only 210 miles (340 kilometers). Two-thirds of the continent can therefore be described as lying "near the coast." Europe's coastlines assume many forms: steep and flat coasts; skerry and fjord coasts in northern Europe; sandbar and lagoon coasts along the Baltic Sea; "watt" or mudflat coasts along the North Sea; rias coasts in the Mediterranean region; and deltas at the mouths of the Rhone, Po, and Danube Rivers.

Europe's average elevation is 984 feet (300 meters), making it the Earth's lowest-lying continent. Although it is located outside of the tropics between 37 and 71 degrees North latitude, it does not rank among the colder continents, but belongs instead to the world's more temperate and densely settled continents. Its temperate climate results from the influence of the warm Gulf Stream in the North Atlantic.

Morphological, tectonic, climatic, and historical factors subdivide the continent. Recent chains of high mountain like the Pyrenees, Alps, Dinaric Alps, and Balkan Mountains set apart southern Europe, which derives its character from its rainy winter climate and from historical and cultural developments in the Mediterranean region. The Dinaric and Carpathian arc extends to the Black Sea and encloses southeastern Europe. The Atlantic Ocean influences the climate and history of western Europe, including the British Isles. A gradual transition between western and central Europe occurs in the Rhine region. The northern German lowlands extend to the eastern European lowlands. Eastern Europe is characterized by the flatness and uniformity of its land, where topographic differences seldom exceed 660 feet (200 meters) in height, by the "wide open spaces," and by the extremes of its continental climate. Northern Europe includes Iceland with its volcanoes and glaciers, the Scandinavian peninsula and Finland, and Denmark.

# Europe: Settlement Patterns and Ec

# omic Regions

### Settlement Patterns and Economic Regions, Depicted in Terms of Light Sources

☐ light sources

Along with the high percentage of which islands and peninsulas comprise its total area and its location in the temperate middle latitudes, Europe's other distinguishing characteristics include an abundance of extensive lowlands and a relatively small percentage of high and medium-high mountains. These natural conditions are partly responsible for the distribution of populations across the entire continent.

Measuring instruments aboard the satellite detect points of light on the surface below. These bright spots indicate the locations of human settlements as well as the distribution of manufacturing sites. That's why this image also shows the sites of refineries, even though such installations are usually situated in sparsely settled locations.

The points of light are arranged according to certain guidelines. Chains of light tend to follow coastlines: this reflects the coastal orientation of human populations and their tendency to congregate in harbor cities. Also, the sources of light follow the familiar courses of major rivers and transportation axes – the Upper Rhine Valley (Switzerland and Germany), the Po River plain (Italy), and (with large gaps) the Danube (first of all Germany and Austria). The largest continuous band of light radiates from the region of agglomeration stretching from the northern edge of Germany's Mittelgebirge (central mountains), across the Ruhr region, Holland, and Belgium, through the Greater London metropolitan area, and into the industrial areas of central England. Compared to that nearly uninterrupted streak, other points of light gleam like isolated diamonds: the Spanish capital of Madrid in the center of the Iberian peninsula; Paris, the heart of France; Moscow, in the midst of the broad eastern European lowlands; and St. Petersburg, shimmering like a far-northern star.

These points of light also provide clues about relatively sparsely settled parts of Europe. Mountain ranges are particularly striking: the dark Alps, surrounded by their gleaming wreath of city lights; the dark arc of the Carpathian Mountains in the southeast part of Central Europe; and the long pale line of the mountains in Scandinavia. Certain agriculturally cultivated plains are likewise dark and sparsely populated. The forest cover of northern Europe appears as a dark region. Other thinly settled areas include many islands with no industries – Iceland, Ireland, Sardinia, Corsica, and Crete.

# Digital Topographic Model of Europe

**Depth Below Mean Sea Level**

| | |
|---|---|
| ■ | more than 19,700 feet |
| ■ | 19,700 – 13,100 feet |
| ■ | 13,100 – 9,800 feet |
| ■ | 9,800 – 6,600 feet |
| ■ | 6,600 – 3,300 feet |
| ■ | 3,300 – 1,600 feet |
| ■ | 1,600 – 650 feet |
| ■ | 650 – 0 feet |

**Elevations Above Mean Sea Level**

| | |
|---|---|
| ■ | 0 feet |
| ■ | 0 – 82 feet |
| ■ | 82 – 165 feet |
| ■ | 165 – 330 feet |
| ■ | 330 – 660 feet |
| ■ | 650 – 1,600 feet |
| ■ | 1,600 – 3,300 feet |
| ■ | 3,300 – 4,900 feet |
| ■ | 4,900 – 6,600 feet |
| ■ | 6,600 – 9,800 feet |
| ■ | 9,800 – 16,400 feet |
| ■ | more than 16,400 feet |

A depiction of the distribution of elevations in Europe clearly reveals the continent's morphological and tectonic composition. A framework of mountains in the south, northwest, and northeast surrounds a broad block of lowlands that opens toward the east. The 660-foot (200-meter) depth line more or less coincides with the edge of the continental shelf and thus with the actual boundary between continent and ocean. The Baltic Shield with the depression of the Baltic Sea continues as flat tablelands toward the Ural and Caucasus mountains. The terrain rises toward the folded Caledonian mountains of Scandinavia, Scotland, and Ireland, and also ascends toward the variscite hills and mountainous lands of central Europe. The Mediterranean Sea is subdivided into individual basins, some of which represent the remnants of the primordial Tethys Ocean, which shrank as Africa drifted northward.

# Digital Topographic Model of the Alp.

**Elevations** (above mean sea level)

|  |  |  |
|---|---|---|
| 0 – 820 feet | 2,500 – 3,300 feet | 8,200 – 9,800 feet |
| 820 – 1,600 feet | 3,300 – 4,900 feet | more than 9,800 feet |
| 1,600 – 2,500 feet | 4,900 – 6,600 feet |  |
|  | 6,600 – 8,200 feet |  |

The elevations of the Alps and their surrounding lands are depicted in individual steplike levels. This view emphasizes the boundaries, rugged terrain, and internal subdivisions of this geologically youthful high-mountain region. Longitudinal and transverse valleys subdivide the Alps, separate mountain massifs and mountain ranges, trace the trough valleys that the alpine valley glaciers once filled as they flowed from the central Alps into the foothills, and show the tectonically determined lines followed by settlements and overland transportation routes.

# Avalanche at Bischofsmütze

On September 22, 1993, a terrific roar accompanied the plunge of 1.8 million cubic feet (50,000 cubic meters) of rock plummeting from the eastern face of the 8,068-foot (2,459-meter) tall Grosse Bischofsmütze in Austria. On the morning of October 10, 1993, another mighty avalanche occurred as some 3.5 million cubic feet (100,000 cubic meters) of stone plunged from the mountain's southern face. The avalanche of stone struck weathered strata that covered the dolomite stone below the cliffs; the impact sent a dense cloud of dust into the air. When the dust cleared, the niche from which the stone had fallen and the pile of fresh debris became visible.

Bischofsmütze is one of the most strikingly shaped mountains in the northern Kalkalpen. Part of the Dachstein group, it is composed mostly of Triassic limestone and dolomite and forms large, karstic, waterless high planes, above which tower individual rugged peaks like the Grosse Bischofsmütze.

Austrian geologists have researched these events and identified several causes leading to these avalanches. The geological structure is the most significant precondition. Massive and brittle Dachstein limestone, of which the peaks of the Kleine and Grosse Bischofsmütze are made, rests atop a base made of dolomite. Both of these types of stone have been subjected to severe weathering since the Ice Age. Vertical gaps developed in the limestone cliffs, and these gaps were subsequently widened into cave-like shapes by rain and meltwater. Over millions of years, clay became deposited in these caves. Clay shrinks when it dries and swells again when it is moistened. This alternation between shrinking and swelling loosens the cliff's structure. In addition, the cliff's limestone walls lose their solid foundation when the dolomite crumbles away.

After a long period of rain and cold weather, the cliff was subjected to strong sunshine on a föhn day – the day of the avalanche. The abrupt warming of the stone, pressure in the water-filled gaps, and swelling of the clay inside those gaps caused the already loosened parts of the wall to break free and plunge into the basin-shaped valley.

Because of fissuring prevalent in this karst landscape, the Bischofsmütze has been compared to a decaying, slowly crumbling tooth. Future avalanches are likely.

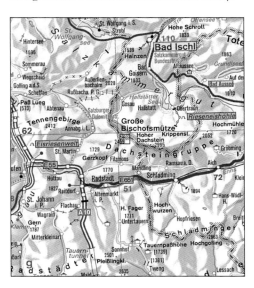

Scale of the map segment: 1 to 800,000

0    8    16    24    32    40 km

0    8    16    24    30 Statute Miles

# The Aletsch Glacier

The satellite photo is divided diagonally into three landscapes. Several massifs and mountain chains belonging to the Bernese Alps (Switzerland) are visible in the northern part of the photo, including the 14,022-foot (4,274-meter) Finsteraarhorn and the 13,642-foot (4,158-meter) Jungfrau as the highest peaks. In the south, are the Wallisian Alps along the Swiss-Italian border. The middle of the picture is occupied by the broad Rhone Valley, known as "Goms" in its uppermost segment. The Alps' largest expanses of ice are found in these two massifs. Their characteristics are firn fields, which feed the glaciers, and valley glaciers at lower elevations where the ice begins to melt. These dissimilar surfaces each influence the type of glaciation, which also depends on the topography of each individual region. These are also known as "alpine" glaciers.

In the Bernese Alps, several glaciers flow out of armchair-shaped hollows (called "karen") in the steep cliff faces and join in a flat firn field at Konkordiaplatz. Ice in this firn basin reaches a thickness of 2,600 feet (790 meters). Konkordiaplatz is also the source of the Alps' longest stream of ice, the Great Aletsch Glacier (north central portion of photo), which flows toward the valley in a 15-mile (24-kilometer)-long arc at a speed of 656 feet (200 meters) per year. The 46-square-mile (120-square-kilometer) surface of this stream of ice, whose maximum width measures 600 feet (1,800 meters), is marked with the longitudinal stripes of its medial moraines. Until a few decades ago, the Middle and Upper Aletsch Glaciers still flowed into the Great Aletsch Glacier from the right. That they no longer do so is symptomatic of the retreat widely

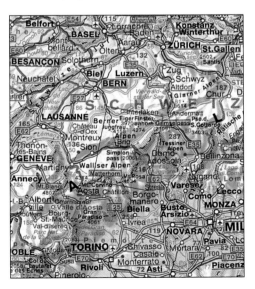

observed in all alpine glaciers and is probably a consequence of climatic warming.

South of the Finsteraarhorn, at the steep southern declivity of the Bernese Alps, the Fiescher Glacier pushes its way down the valley. The debris-laden Unteraar Glacier and the Rhone Glacier, whose meltwaters are the source of the Rhone River, fill the valley near Grimsel and Furka (northeastern corner of the photo).

Toward the north, several brooks drain the mountain massif as they descend toward Lake Thun and the Lake of Brienz. Glaciers carved the more than 656-foot (200-meter)-deep basins of these lakes during the Ice Ages as they scraped through existing depressions on their way down to the foothills.

The Gorner Glacier can be seen on the northern flank of the Monte Rosa Group in the Wallisian Alps. Eight miles (13 kilometers) long and with a surface area of more than 23 square miles (60 square kilometers), Gorner Glacier is the Alps' second largest valley glacier. At the southern edge of the photo, the 14,692-foot (4,478-meter) tall Matterhorn casts its shadow across the northern firn fields. Its steep rock faces were

*A view from Eggishorn of the Great Aletsch Glacier (Switzerland) showing the striped pattern of its medial moraines. Ice-free trough slopes and shoulders on the mountain's flanks suggest that the glacier attained higher elevations in the past.*

formed during the Ice Ages, when "karen" ate away at this peak from several sides simultaneously.

The shape of the Rhone Valley is likewise due to Ice Age glaciation. At that time, a mighty glacier flowed through the not yet glaciated Rhone Valley, scraping and deepening it to create a wide trough with steep walls and moderately eroded shoulders. After the Ice Age, the river deposited its debris along the valley floor, thus creating the valley's present flat profile. The main valley continues to receive detritus from the Rhones tributaries, which flow through lateral valleys, cut sharply into the trough's sides, and deposit their load as alluvial fans along the trough's walls. Green expanses of alpine pastures are visible at elevations between 5,000 and 6,500 feet (1,500 and 2,000 meters).

Fruit and wine are cultivated up to considerable elevations on sunny slopes with southern exposures; the trough valley's shoulders are also cultivated as irrigated fields. Irrigation is necessary here because the Wallis is one of the Alps' sunniest valleys.

Scale of the map segment: 1 to 4,000,000

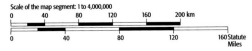

0   40   80   120   160   200 km

0   40   80   120   160 Statute Miles

# Europe's Network of Waterways

**Network of Waterways**

 river

lake

salt-pan, salt lake

This satellite-generated pictorial map shows Europe's ground cover and the courses of its larger rivers. The catchment areas of the seas surrounding Europe vary both in size and in the degree to which they extend into the continent. The various rivers' runoff behavior depends on the annual rhythms of precipitation and condensation as well as - amount of snow, which either remains frozen or melts and swells the rivers.

Much of Eastern Europe is drained by the Volga River, whose mouth lies at the Caspian Sea. With a total length of 2,175 miles (3,500 kilometers), the Volga is Europe's longest river. It also boasts by far the largest catchment area, draining some 525 square miles (1,360 square kilometers). Dammed at many points, the Volga is linked by canals, with the Baltic and Black Seas. Other rivers that cross the eastern European lowlands include the Don (1,160 miles = 1,870 kilometers; the Dnieper (1,367 miles = 2,200 kilometers); and the Dniester. Compared to these long rivers, the eastern and middle European rivers that empty into the Baltic Sea have comparatively small catchment areas and are relatively short: the Vistula (651 miles = 1,047 kilometers), the Odra (531 miles = 854 kilometers), the Klaipeda, and the Düna.

The Danube, Europe's second longest river, originates in the Black Forest in Germany, bends toward the east, passes through several mountain ranges, absorbs other rivers draining the Alps, Carpathian, and the Sudetic Mountains, flows across the lowlands of southern Europe, and finally empties through its delta in Rumania into the Black Sea after a journey of 1,770 miles (2,850 kilometers).

All other central and western European rivers drain into either the North Sea or the Atlantic Ocean. Most are navigable for many miles upstream. Important port cities have been built along the shores of several of these rivers.

Because of the dryness in summer and the consequently drastic fluctuations in their water levels, most of southern Europe's rivers are not navigable. The exception is the Po River in Italy, which flows between levees across the flat Po Plain.

Lakes are visible as large, dark expanses: Lake Ladoga (6,834 square miles = 17,700 square kilometers) and Lake Onega (3,750 square miles = 9,720 square kilometers) in the northeast; the comparatively small Lake Balaton in Hungary (228 square miles = 591 square kilometers); and the small lakes along the edges of the Alps, which include Lake Geneva in Switzerland (224 square miles = 581 square kilometers) and Lake Constance (208 square miles = 538 square kilometers), which borders on Germany, Austria and Switzerland.

# The Netherlands: Battling the Ocean and Floods

The history of the Netherlands is the epic tale of a thousand-year battle against the sea. Again and again, catastrophic storm floods have devastated the country, but the Dutch have repeatedly persevered and won back their land.

The components of a flat tidal coastline are lined up here in a typical series. The "frontline" in this struggle with the sea is a natural dike formed by a belt of dunes up to 200 feet (60 meters) in height. These dunes have survived undestroyed in northern Holland (southwestern corner of photo), but are interrupted in several places in the vicinity of the Wadden Islands. The amphibious area of the Wadden Zee, with its tidal gullies, is completely closed off from the sea by a straight line of dikes. Behind the line of dikes, systems of drainage canals and bucket elevators are used to create polders by draining marshes that sometimes lie well below sea level.

In 1260, the sea stormed into the area of what is now the IJsselmeer and devastated the countryside. In 1894 the Dutch parliament decided to enact the Ijsselmeer Project. The dike separating the IJsselmeer from the Wadden Zee was raised between 1926 and 1932; the first two IJsselmeer polders (Wierigermeer and Nordost Polder) were completed and connected to the mainland in 1930 and 1942, respectively. In contrast, the polders of East and South Flevoland (1957 and 1968) were kept isolated from the mainland in order to maintain adequately high levels of ground water in sandy heathland areas.

The planned Markerwaard Polder was fully enclosed by dikes by the beginning of the 1980s, but Dutch spatial planning goals had changed in the meantime. In the past, protecting the coast from flooding and gaining more land for agriculture and settlement had been the highest priorities. Nowadays, nature conservation, water management, and recreational uses are becoming increasingly significant. Markerwaard Polder was therefore not completed as planned, but is now used as a freshwater reservoir, fish basin, and site for water sports.

*This multicolored photo was created by compiling data from several different points in time: blue (September 21, 1994), green (January 30, 1995), and red (February 5, 1995). Severe flooding, which swelled the Rhine,* *Waal, and Maas Rivers in late January 1995 is a reminder that the Netherlands are not only endangered by the ocean, but that the nation's low-lying polders are also vulnerable to flooding from the continent.*

Scale of the map segment: 1 to 4,000,000

| 0 | 40 | 80 | 120 | 160 | 200 km |

| 0 | 40 | 80 | 120 | 160 Statute Miles |

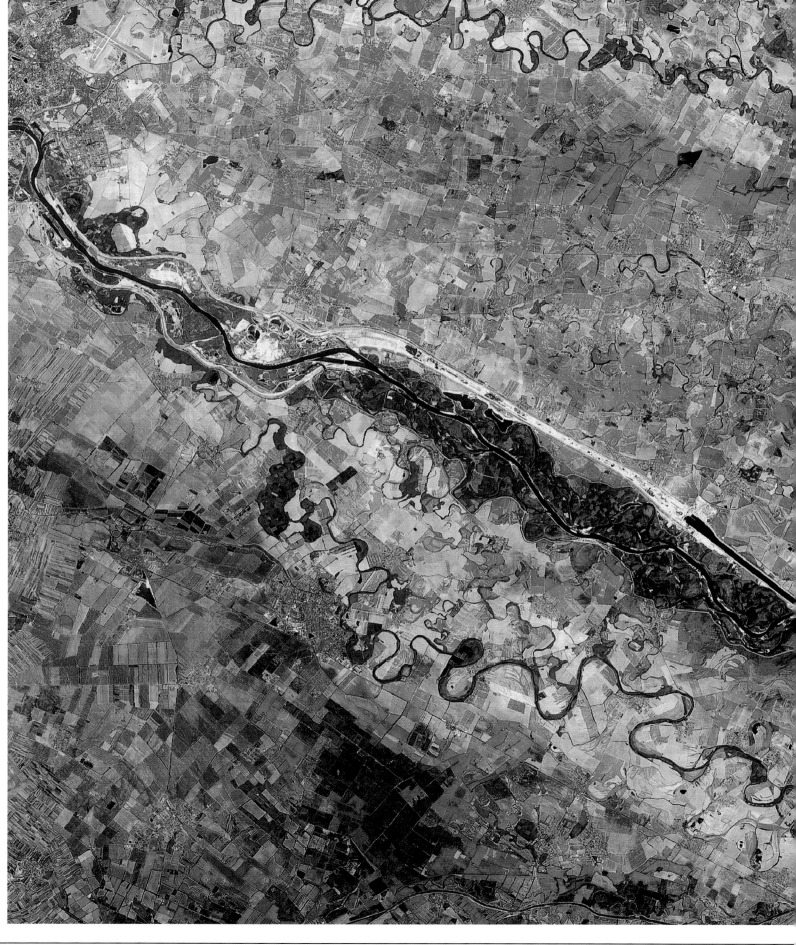

# A Hydraulic Engineering Project in the Danube River

This satellite photo shows a section of the Danube landscape between Bratislava in the northwest and Gyor in the southeast, where the three countries of Austria, the Slovak Republic, and Hungary meet. The Austrian-Hungarian border runs close to the western edge of the picture, and can be indirectly discerned by looking at the various forms and sizes of the plots of land. The Hungarian agricultural cooperatives' large block-shaped fields stand in marked contrast to the small fields of private farms in Austria. The border between Hungary and the Slovak Republic follows the course of the Danube. A multitude of serpentine backwaters surrounds Danube's present riverbed. The Kis-Danube meanders along the northern edge of the photo, as does the Moson-Danube in the south. Both of these rivers are subsidiary branches of the Danube, which deposited Europe's largest river island here at the end of the Ice Age. These two tributaries join the Danube's main channel below Gyor.

The so-called Old Danube runs diagonally through the photo. Its gravel banks are readily visible.

The large, light-colored, mostly empty canal north of the Old Danube is particularly evident in the photo. Likewise visible are a number of recently built dams that follow the river starting at Bratislava.

All this is part of the bilateral Gabcikovo/Nagymoros hydraulic engineering project, which has been in planning since the 1950s. At the end of 59-foot (18 meter)-tall lateral dams lies Dunakiliti, where a weir will reroute approximately nine-tenths of the Danube's average water flow through an asphalt side canal on Slovakian territory. Gabcikovo hydroelectric plant can be seen in the photo at the dividing line between the empty and full parts of the canal. When completed, it will create a 75-foot (23-meter) waterfall, and will have the world's largest sluice. A storage lake about 68 miles (110 kilometers) in length will stretch upstream from Nagymoros, which lies 9 miles (15 kilometers) above Budapest. This lake will compensate for manmade flood waves of more than 13 feet (4 meters) in height, which will issue from the power plant twice a day.

The two power plants are scheduled to produce a total of 880 megawatts of electricity, which will be divided equally between Hungary and the Slovak Republic. This energy, however, will satisfy less than five percent of Hungary's energy requirements.

Massive protests by environmentalists have temporarily delayed the project. The plan's opponents argue that its implementation would:

– lead to deposition of toxic sediments in the dammed bodies of water, which would pollute drinking water currently obtained by filtering water from the river;

– increase the growth of algae in the nearly stagnant waters of man-made lakes;

– dry up meadow vegetation along the Old Danube;

– flood Danube's tributaries;

– and overstrain the financial capacities of Hungary and the Slovak Republic.

The project's ultimate fate has not yet been decided. Negotiations are currently underway; some changes in the planned constructions may be agreed upon.

Scale of the map segment: 1 to 2,000,000

# The Distribution of Temperatures an

**Mean Monthly Temperatures**

**Below Freezing**

| | |
|---|---|
| ■ | −4 – +5 °Fahrenheit |
| ■ | +5 – 14 °Fahrenheit |
| ▨ | 14 – 23 °Fahrenheit |
| ▢ | 23 – 32 °Fahrenheit |

**Above Freezing**

| | |
|---|---|
| ▢ | 32 – 41 °Fahrenheit |
| ▢ | 41 – 50 °Fahrenheit |
| ▨ | 50 – 59 °Fahrenheit |
| ▨ | 59 – 68 °Fahrenheit |
| ■ | 68 – 77 °Fahrenheit |
| ▨ | 77 – 86 °Fahrenheit |
| ■ | 86 – 95 °Fahrenheit |

Mean Monthly Temperature: Summer

Mean Monthly Temperature: Winter

# Precipitation in Europe

**Mean Monthly Precipitation**

| | |
|---|---|
| | less than 0.4 inches |
| | 0.4 – 2.0 inches |
| | 2.0 – 4.0 inches |
| | 4.0 – 8.0 inches |
| | 8.0 – 16.0 inches |
| | more than 16 inches |

Mean Monthly Precipitation: Summer

Mean Monthly Precipitation: Winter

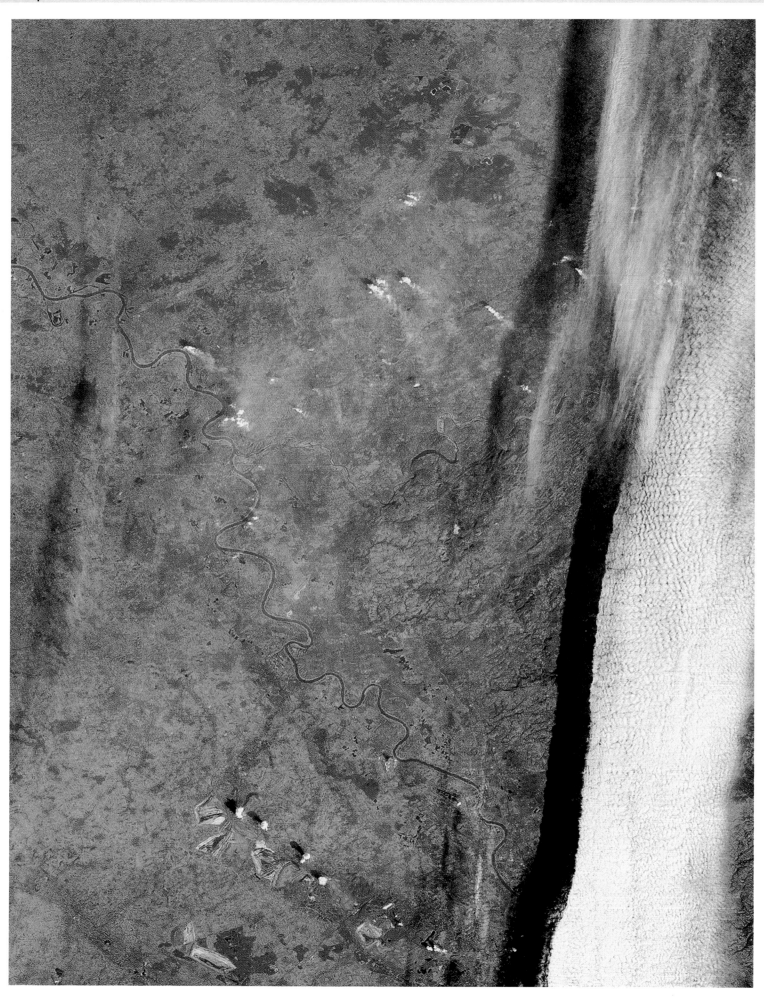

# Air Pollution in the Ruhr Region

A broad band of stratus clouds hides the terrain east of Cologne in Germany along the picture's eastern edge, but the rest of the sky is free of clouds. Nothing obscures one's view of even the smallest details in this densely settled industrial area of North Rhine-Westphalia (Nordrhein-Westfalen), except the clouds of smoke rising from power plants' cooling towers.

Two axes of concentration are visible. An urbanized strip stretches along the Rhine from Cologne to Düsseldorf, across Duisburg/Rheinhausen with the Mannesmann steel works and Ruhrorter harbor, through Hamborn with the Thyssen AG's industrial installations and from Walsum to Wesel. In its narrow sense, the phrase "Ruhr Region" includes the intensively developed area between the Ruhr River in the south and the Emscher. The cities here – Oberhausen, Essen, Gelsenkirchen, Bochum, and Dortmund – all lie along an ancient trade route linking the Rhine with Paderborn during the Germanic era. These cities, once the sites of coal mines, follow the direction of the coal veins and underground coal deposits within the mountain range.

As mining moved into the Lippe and northern Emscher zone, anthracite-coal-fueled power plants likewise resettled farther north. Their plumes of smoke point toward the southeast, where the terrain ascends into the Sauerland. Forests on the windward slopes of these mountains are severely damaged.

Because of industrial restructuring in the Ruhr Region following the coal and steel crisis (beginning in 1958), the volume of pollutant emissions (especially sulfur dioxide) has been reduced by more than 80 percent. The number of greenbelts, recreation areas, and athletic fields has increased.

These environmental improvements have not been correspondingly dramatic in the Rhineland's brown-coal region. When winds are still, towering cumulus clouds of steam rise above brown-coal mining activities in the Ville-Erftal region west of Cologne (in the southwestern part of the picture), where tectonic uplift has raised the Ville's brown-coal deposits close to the surface. Plumes of smoke are created when raw brown coal is dried in the power plants; these plumes indicate the location of the plants near open-pit coal mines. The magnitude of landscape destruction is unmistakable. Long shadows cast in the terraced open-pit mines hint at the tremendous depth of these excavations (more than 980 feet = 300 meters).

An unbroken layer of clouds covers the densely populated industrial region of Rhine-Westphalia in Germany. An extended period of cold winter weather can lead to atmospheric stagnation: a layer of warm air rests atop a stratum of colder air near the ground. Tall smokestacks penetrate upward and release their emissions at fairly high altitudes, but the temperature inversion prevents smoke and effluent gases from dissipating. Smog threatens.

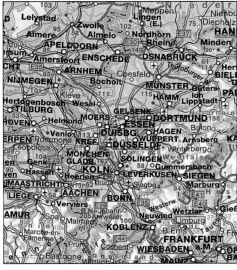

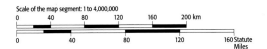

Scale of the map segment: 1 to 4,000,000

0   40   80   120   160   200 km

0        40        80        120        160 Statute Miles

# Air Pollution Caused by Air Traffic

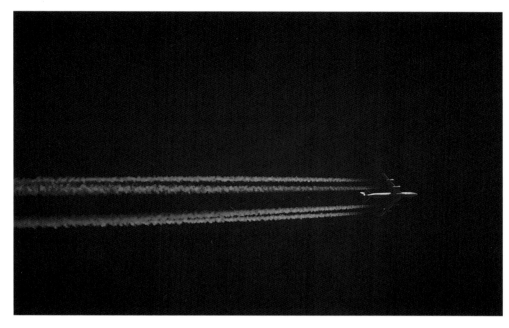

*Skies above Central Europe are seldom free of contrails. These manmade ice clouds condense from the water vapor produced during the combustion of airplane fuel. Contrails contain large amounts of toxic substances, similar to those present in the exhaust produced by road vehicles. The congested air traffic over Central Europe significantly contributes to air pollution and the greenhouse effect.*

High-altitude condensation fields appear red in this false-color satellite photograph. This coloring emphasizes the area of fleecy clouds in the southeastern corner and, above all, the mostly southwest to northeast orientation of the broad stripes of the condensation trails left in the wake of airplanes. Fuhlsbüttel, Hamburg's international airport, one of the most important in Germany, is located beneath the point where these contrails are the densest. The southern part of the satellite photo is almost free of contrails because the layers of air there were either too turbulent or too warm to permit them to form at the time when this photo was taken. Contrails only remain visible at temperatures between −58 and −94 degrees Fahrenheit (−50 and −70 degrees Celsius).

Many of these contrails were undoubtedly caused by military airplanes: on the one hand, the concentration of military airfields is especially high in Schleswig-Holstein and Lower Saxony; on the other hand, the orientation of the visible trails does not coincide with the flight routes used by civilian air traffic in this region.

Airplanes are the most energy-intensive form of transportation. Nearly 3.3 million short tons (3 million metric tons) of airplane fuel are consumed each year within German airspace. Burning that much fuel creates above all carbon dioxide (9.6 million short tons = 8.7 million metric tons above Germany), water vapor (3.7 million short tons = 3.4 million metric tons), carbon monoxide (53,000 short tons = 48,000 metric tons), nitrogen oxide (32,000 short tons = 29,000 metric tons), hydrocarbons (9,920 short tons = 9,000 metric tons), and sulfur dioxide (2,980 short tons = 2,700 metric tons). Although airplane exhausts comprise only about 1 percent of the entire volume of emissions released by the various forms of transportation, their effects are at least as serious as those caused by street traffic because airplanes release their pollutants high above the Earth's surface. International air traffic flies at altitudes above 33,000 feet (10 kilometers). Physicochemical conditions at those altitudes differ markedly from conditions at ground level, which is why air-traffic emissions attain very high concentrations and persist for such a long time. The strong ultraviolet radiation at these heights converts nitrogen oxides emitted by airplanes into ozone. Higher up – at altitudes of about 50,000 feet (15 kilometers) – ozone is being destroyed. The volume of carbon dioxide emitted by airplanes contributes to the warming of the atmosphere.

Even more problematic, however, is the water vapor that, at such low temperatures, immediately condenses into ice crystals.

Condensation trails scarcely hinder incident solar radiation, but they do significantly reduce the rate of radiant cooling of the ground surface. According to a NASA computer simulation, a mere two-percent increase in ice clouds would raise the Earth's average temperature by 1.8 degrees Fahrenheit (1 degree Celsius).

Three measures are urgently needed: a significant reduction in short-haul air traffic; establishment of pollutant-level limits for airplane exhausts; and a prohibition barring flights above the troposphere (higher than approximately 33,000 feet = 10 kilometers).

Scale of the map segment: 1 to 4,000,000

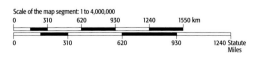

# Damaged Forests in the Ore Mountains

The satellite photo shows several landscapes, all of which run in a southwest-northeast direction parallel to the Ore Mountains (Germany and the Czech Republic). The center of the picture is occupied by the Ore Mountains with their gently declining northern slopes (into which the Elbe's left-hand tributaries have dug their valleys) and their steep southern slopes (which descend abruptly toward the northern Bohemian Basin). Bohemia's central mountains enter the picture farther south, adjoined by the valley of the Eger. The Elbe appears as a linear element linking these landscapes with one another. Its serpentine channel traverses Bohemia's agricultural lands. The forests that once covered the hills here were cut down long ago. The Elbe is joined by the Eger, breaks first through the Bohemian central mountains (whose upper reaches are still covered by forests), and then through the Elbe sandstone mountains. The sandstone tablelands of the Swiss Saxony with their uniquely shaped cliffs and mountains are still mostly wooded. North of here, the Elbe is joined by the rivers that drain the Ore Mountain's northern slopes (which are still covered with a few scattered patches of forest) and enters the wider portion of its valley in the Dresden region. Poor ventilation in this basin allows air-pollution levels to rise (violet shades).

The Ore Mountains were entirely wooded in the remote past; their forest cover was still mostly intact until a few decades ago. Only in the immediate vicinity of the ore deposits had the forest been cleared. Cutting began in the 12th century. Nowadays, this formerly wooded mountain range is a landscape devoid of trees. The forest has almost entirely disappeared from the mountains' ridges; remaining patches of forest are severely damaged for as much as 12 miles (20 kilometers) down the northern slopes.

We now know that the death of the forests stems from the interaction of several contributing causes. Air pollution is the chief culprit. The satellite photo documents this situation.

Northern Bohemia's brown-coal region, whose eastern portion lies hidden beneath cloud cover, has been ruthlessly exploited for raw materials and energy resources since World War II. Here in this heavily industrialized and densely populated region, brown coal (which contains high concentrations of sulfur) is mined and then burned as the chief source of fuel in heating plants erected beside open-pit mines. Local and global air currents transport the toxins elsewhere. Acid rain and the deleterious effects of sulfur dioxide have severely damaged the forests, especially those growing on the acid soil of the Ore Mountains. Another source of devastation is the chemical industry, which spews more than 1.1 million short tons (1 million metric tons) of sulfur dioxide into the air each year and whose waste heaps release some 310,000 short tons (280,000 metric tons) of dust particles into the atmosphere. Because of the location in the lee of the Ore Mountains, winds here can mix and whirl pollutants about but can only carry off a very small percentage. All of the forested areas in northern Bohemia's brown-coal region are either dead or severely damaged. Especially the more sensitive species of trees in the Ore Mountains and in the northern Bohemian Basin – firs, spruces, pines and beeches –are already dead.

Ruined forests in the Ore Mountains (Germany and the Czech Republic) near Oberwiesenthal: these forests died so quickly that foresters could hardly keep pace and haul away the dead trees. Reforestation efforts are currently underway: large expanses of dead forest are cut; fertilizers are judiciously applied; and a diverse spectrum of saplings are sown. It is hoped that this mix of species will be better able to survive the conditions here than were the spruce monocultures.

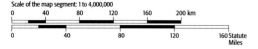

Scale of the map segment: 1 to 4,000,000

0    40    80    120    160    200 km

0    40    80    120    160 Statute Miles

# Glossary

**abiotic** Nonliving.

**adiabatic** Of, relating to, or denoting a reversible thermodynamic process executed at constant entropy and occurring without gain or loss of heat.

**air mass** A large body of air with only small horizontal variations of temperature, pressure, and moisture.

**alpidic fold zone** An area of the Alpine region where oceanic plates are moving beneath continental plates and where one convergent plate collides with another.

**anthropogenic** Relating to the influence humans have on nature.

**aphelion** The point on the orbit of a celestial body that is farthest from the sun.

**atoll** A ringlike coral island and reef that nearly, or entirely, encloses a lagoon.

**avalanche** A fall or slide of a large mass, such as snow or rock, down a mountainside.

**barchan** A dune in the shape of a crescent, the convex side facing the prevailing wind, moved slowly by wind.

**Beaufort Scale** A scale on which successive ranges of wind velocities are assigned code numbers from 0 (calm) to 12 (hurricane), corresponding to wind speeds of from less than 1 mile per hour (0–1 kilometer per hour) to over 74 miles per hour (over 117 kilometers per hour).

**biotic** Of or having to do with life or living organisms.

**catchment** A structure, such as a basin or reservoir, used for collecting or draining water, including rainwater.

**chernozem** A very black topsoil, rich in humus, typical of cool to temperate semiarid regions, such as the grasslands of European Russia.

**chlorofluorocarbon** Abbr. **CFC** Any of various halocarbon compounds consisting of carbon, hydrogen, chlorine, and fluorine, once used widely as aerosol propellants and refrigerants. Chlorofluorocarbons are believed to cause depletion of the atmospheric ozone layer.

**chlorophyll** Any of a group of related green pigments found in photosynthetic organisms.

**climatic zone** Classifications of climate divided into latitudinal zones based on the significant parallels.

**coniferous** Quality of mostly evergreen trees and plants bearing cones.

**continental drift** The movement, formation, or re-formation of continents described by the theory of plate tectonics.

**continental shelf** A submerged border of a continent that slopes gradually and extends to a point of steeper descent to the ocean bottom.

**contrail** A visible condensation of water droplets or ice crystals from the atmosphere occuring in the wake of an aircraft, rocket, or missile under certain conditions.

**coral reef** An erosion-resistant marine ridge or mound consisting chiefly of compacted coral together with algal material and biochemically deposited magnesium and calcium carbonates.

**Coriolis force** An apparent force used mathematically to describe motion, as of aircraft or cloud formations, relative to a noninertial, uniformly rotating frame of reference such as Earth.

**current** The part of a body of liquid or gas that has a continuous onward movement.

**cyclone** An atmospheric system characterized by the rapid, inward circulation of air masses around a low-pressure center, usually accompanied by stormy, often destructive, weather. Cyclones circulate counterclockwise in the Northern Hemisphere and clockwise in the Southern Hemisphere.

**dam** A barrier constructed across a waterway to control the flow or raise the level of water.

**deciduous** Falling off or shed at a specific season or stage of growth. Shedding or losing foliage at the end of the growing season

**desertification** The transformation of arable or habitable land to desert, as by a change in climate or destructive land use.

**dike** An embankment of earth and rock built to prevent floods.

**Dobson unit** A scale for measuring the total amount of ozone occupying a column overhead.

**dune** A hill or ridge of windblown sand.

**eclipse** The partial or complete obscuring, relative to a designated observer, of one celestial body by another.

**ecosystem** An ecological community together with its environment, functioning as a unit.

**effluent** Flowing out or forth.

**El Niño** A warming of the ocean surface off the western coast of South America that occurs every 4 to 12 years when upwelling of cold, nutrient-rich water does not occur. It causes plankton and fish to die and affects weather over much of the Pacific Ocean.

**endogenous** Produced or growing from within.

**Equator** The imaginary great circle around the earth's surface, equidistant from the poles and perpendicular to the earth's axis of rotation. It divides the earth into the Northern Hemisphere and the Southern Hemisphere.

**erosion** The group of natural processes, including weathering, dissolution, abrasion, corrosion, and transportation, by which material is worn away from the earth's surface.

**eutrophication** Process by which waters (usually a lake or pond) become rich in mineral and organic nutrients that promote a proliferation of plant life, especially algae, which reduces the dissolved oxygen content and often causes the extinction of other organisms.

**fault** A fracture in the crust of a planet or moon accompanied by a displacement of one side of the fracture with respect to the other side, usually in a direction parallel to the fracture.

**fault zone** An area containing many small faults.

**flood tide** The incoming or rising tide; the period between low water and the succeeding high water.

**föhn** A warm, dry south wind that blows down the leeward slope of a mountain, especially in the Alps.

**fossil fuel** A hydrocarbon deposit, such as petroleum, coal, or natural gas, derived from living matter of a previous geologic time and used for fuel.

**glacier** A huge mass of ice slowly flowing over a land mass, formed from compacted snow in an area where snow accumulation exceeds melting and sublimation.

**greenhouse effect** The phenomenon whereby the earth's atmosphere traps solar radiation, caused by the presence in the atmosphere of gases such as carbon dioxide, water vapor, and methane that allow incoming sunlight to pass through but absorb heat radiated back from the earth's surface.

**Gulf Stream** A warm ocean current of the northern Atlantic Ocean off eastern North America. It flows from the Gulf of Mexico through the Straits of Florida and then north and northeast to merge with the North Atlantic Drift.

**hemisphere** Either the northern or southern half of the earth as divided by the equator or the eastern or western half as divided by a meridian.

**highland** Elevated land. A mountainous or hilly section of a country.

**holograph** A manuscript or document created without the use of lenses in which a three-dimensional image is recorded on a photographic plate or film by means of laser light.

**horse latitudes** Either of two belts of latitudes located over the oceans at about 30 ° to 35 ° north and south, having high barometric pressure, calms, and light, changeable winds.

**hot spot** An area of intense heat, radiation, or activity.

**hurricane** A severe tropical cyclone originating in the equatorial regions of the Atlantic Ocean or Caribbean Sea, traveling north, northwest, or northeast from its point of origin, and usually involving heavy rains. A wind with a speed greater than 74 miles (119 kilometers) per hour, according to the Beaufort scale.

**hydrology** The scientific study of the properties, distribution, and effects of water on the earth's surface, in the soil and underlying rocks, and in the atmosphere.

**irrigate** To supply (dry land) with water by means of ditches, pipes, or streams; water artificially.

**isohyet** A line drawn on a map connecting points that receive equal amounts of rainfall.

**"karen"** Hollows in rocks, especially the face of a cliff.

**karst/karstic** An area of irregular limestone in which erosion has produced fissures, sinkholes, underground streams, and caverns.

**katabatic** Of or relating to a cold flow of air traveling downward.

**landmass** A large unbroken area of land.

**lapillus** A small, solidified fragment of lava.

**latifundium** A great landed estate, especially of the ancient Romans.

**latitude** The angular distance north or south of the earth's equator, measured in degrees along a meridian, as on a map or globe.

**latosol** Soil that is rich in iron, alumina, or silica and formed in tropical woodlands under a very humid climate with relatively high temperature.

**lava** Molten rock that reaches the earth's surface through a volcano or fissure.

**longitude** Angular distance on the earth's surface, measured east or west from the prime meridian at Greenwich, England, to the meridian passing through a position, expressed in degrees (or hours), minutes, and seconds.

**lowland** An area of land that is low in relation to the surrounding country.

**magma** The molten rock material under the earth's crust, from which igneous rock is formed by cooling.

**massif (mountain)** A large mountain mass or compact group of connected mountains forming an independent portion of a range.

**meltwater** Water from melted ice or snow.

**monsoon** A wind system that influences large climatic regions and reverses direction seasonally.

**moraine** An accumulation of boulders, stones, or other debris carried and deposited by a glacier.

**morphology** The external structure of rocks in relation to the development of erosional forms or topographic features.

**oasis** A fertile or green spot in a desert or wasteland, made so by the presence of water.

**Oya Schio** Japanese, also called **Kuril current,** a surface oceanic current flowing southwest along the Kamchatka Peninsula and the Kuril Islands.

**ozone layer/ozone hole** A region of the upper atmosphere, between about 15 and 30 kilometers (10 and 20 miles) in altitude, containing a relatively high concentration of ozone that absorbs solar ultraviolet radiation in a wavelength range not screened by other atmospheric components.

**pedology** The scientific study of soils, including their origins, characteristics, and uses.

**perihelion** The point nearest the sun in the orbit of a planet or other celestial body.

**permafrost** Permanently frozen subsoil, occurring throughout the Polar Regions and locally in perennially frigid areas.

**photolysis** Chemical decomposition induced by light or other radiant energy.

**photosynthesis** The process in green plants and certain other organisms by which carbohydrates are synthesized from carbon dioxide and water using light as an energy source. Most forms of photosynthesis release oxygen as a byproduct.

**plate drift** Movement of slabs of the Earth's crusts (plates) caused by the ascending and diverging arms of deep convection currents in the Earth's mantle.

**plate tectonics** A theory of global dynamics having to do with the movement of a small number of semirigid sections of the earth's crust, with seismic activity and volcanism occurring primarily at the margins of these sections. This movement has resulted in continental drift and changes in the shape and size of ocean basins and continents.

**polder** An area of low-lying land, especially in the Netherlands, that has been reclaimed from a body of water and is protected by dikes.

**podzol (podsol)** A leached soil formed mainly in cool, humid climates.

**precipitation** Any form of water, such as rain, snow, sleet, or hail, that falls to the earth's surface.

**radioactive clock** Frequency standard (not for ordinary timekeeping) based on the extremely sharp frequency of the gamma emission (electromagnetic radiation arising from radioactive decay) and absorption in certain atomic nuclei, such as iron-57.

**rain forest** A dense evergreen forest occupying a tropical region with an annual rainfall of at least 2.5 meters (100 inches).

**range** An extended group or series, especially a row or chain of mountains.

**rift valley** A deep fracture or break, about 25–50 km (15–30 miles) wide, extending along the crest of a mid-ocean ridge.

**riparian** Of, on, or relating to the banks of a natural course of water.

**river delta** Low-lying plain that is composed of stream-borne sediments deposited by a river at its mouth.

**Sahel Zone** Arabic "SAHIL," semiarid region of western and north-central Africa extending from Senegal eastward to the Sudan. It forms a transitional zone between the arid Sahara (desert) to the north and the belt of humid savannas to the south.

**salinification** Making salty, as land or water.

**salinity** Of, relating to, or containing salt; salty.

**satellite imagery** Photography or photos taken from an orbiting satellite.

**savanna** A flat grassland of tropical or subtropical regions.

**sclerophyllous** Having leathery leaves that resist easy loss of moisture.

**sea level** The level of the ocean's surface, especially the level halfway between mean high and low tide, used as a standard in reckoning land elevation or sea depths.

**shelf** A projecting ledge of rock or a balcony, that resembles such a structure. A reef, sandbar, or shoal.

**shelf sea** The part of the sea that covers a continental shelf

**snout** A similar prolongation of the anterior portion of the head in certain insects, such as weevils; a rostrum. A spout or nozzle shaped like such a projection.

**steppe** A vast semiarid grass-covered plain, as found in southeast Europe, Siberia, and central North America.

**stratosphere** The region of the atmosphere above the troposphere and below the mesosphere.

**stripe dunes** Elongated lines of sand dunes, formed parallel to the direction of the predominant winds, caused by winds blowing from the same direction for many weeks a year.

**taiga** A subarctic, evergreen coniferous forest of northern Eurasia located just south of the tundra and dominated by firs and spruces.

**tectonics (tectonic theory)** Branch of geology concerned with the structure of the crust of a planet (as Earth) or the moon, especially related to the formation of folds and faults in it.

**tornado** A rotating column of air usually accompanied by a funnel-shaped downward extension of a cumulonimbus cloud and having a vortex several hundred yards in diameter whirling destructively at speeds of up to 500 miles (800 kilometers) per hour.

**trace gas** A gas in minute quantities.

**trade wind** Any of a consistent system of prevailing winds occupying most of the tropics, constituting the major component of the general circulation of the atmosphere, and blowing northeasterly in the Northern Hemisphere and southeasterly in the Southern Hemisphere.

**transverse valley** A valley lying or extending across or in a cross direction.

**tree line** The limit of northern or southern latitude beyond which trees will not grow except as stunted forms.

**Tropic of Cancer** The parallel of latitude 23° 27' north of the equator, the northern boundary of the Torrid Zone, and the most northerly latitude at which the sun can shine directly overhead.

**Tropic of Capricorn** The parallel of latitude 23° 27' south of the equator, the southern boundary of the Torrid Zone, and the most southerly latitude at which the sun can shine directly overhead.

**tropical cyclone** A cyclone originating over tropical oceans, characterized by violent rainstorms and winds with velocities of up to 320 kilometers (200 miles) per hour.

**troposphere** The lowest region of the atmosphere between the earth's surface and the tropopause (the region at the top of the troposphere), characterized by decreasing temperature with increasing altitude.

**tundra** A treeless area between the icecap and the tree line of Arctic regions, having a permanently frozen subsoil and supporting low-growing vegetation such as lichens, mosses, and stunted shrubs.

**umbra** A dark area, especially the blackest part of a shadow from which all light is cut off.

**variscite** A mineral occuring in bright green, crystalline, or kidney-shaped crusts.

**volcanic bomb** A piece of molten lava, often very large and hollow, thrown out of a volcano in eruption.

**wadi** A valley, gully, or streambed in northern Africa and southwest Asia that remains dry except during the rainy season.

**weir** A dam placed across a river or canal to raise or divert the water, as for a millrace, or to regulate or measure the flow.

**windscreen** A screen for protection against the wind. In deserts, rows of tamarisk to reduce wind speeds and slow the movement of sand dunes.

# Index

Note: page numbers in *italics* indicate photographs.

162